Islamic Extremism
and the
War of Ideas

————

Lessons from Indonesia

HERBERT AND JANE DWIGHT WORKING GROUP
ON ISLAMISM AND THE INTERNATIONAL ORDER

Many of the writings associated with this
Working Group will be published by the Hoover Institution.
Materials published to date, or in production, are listed below.

ESSAYS

Saudi Arabia and the New Strategic Landscape
Joshua Teitelbaum

Islamism and the Future of the Christians of the Middle East
Habib C. Malik

Syria through Jihadist Eyes: A Perfect Enemy
Nibras Kazimi

The Ideological Struggle for Pakistan
Ziad Haider

BOOKS

Freedom or Terror: Europe Faces Jihad
Russell A. Berman

*The Myth of the Great Satan:
A New Look at America's Relations with Iran*
Abbas Milani

Torn Country: Turkey between Secularism and Islamism
Zeyno Baran

Islamic Extremism and the War of Ideas: Lessons from Indonesia
John Hughes

Crosswinds: The Way of Saudi Arabia
Fouad Ajami

Islamic Extremism

and the

War of Ideas

Lessons from Indonesia

John Hughes

HOOVER INSTITUTION PRESS

STANFORD UNIVERSITY | STANFORD, CALIFORNIA

www.hoover.org

Hoover Institution Press Publication No. 592

Hoover Institution at Leland Stanford Junior University, Stanford, California, 94305-6010

First printing 2010
16   15   14   13   12   11   10   6   5   4   3   2   1

Manufactured in the United States of America

The paper used in this publication meets the minimum Requirements of the American National Standard for Information Sciences—Permanence of Paper for Printed Library Materials, ANSI/NISO Z39.48-1992. ⊚

Library of Congress Cataloging-in-Publication Data
Hughes, John, 1960–
Islamic extremism and the war of ideas : lessons from Indonesia /
John Hughes.
    p.   cm.
Published in association with the Herbert and Jane Dwight Working Group on Islamism and the International Order.
    Includes bibliographical references and index.
    ISBN 978-0-8179-1164-5 (cloth : alk. paper)—
    ISBN 978-0-8179-1166-9 (e-book)
1. Islam and politics—Indonesia.   2. Indonesia—Politics and government.
3. Islamic fundamentalism—Indonesia.   I. Herbert and Jane Dwight Working Group on Islamism and the International Order.   II. Title.
BP63.I5H79   2010
320.5'5709598—dc22   2010023473

*The Hoover Institution gratefully acknowledges
the following individuals and foundations
for their significant support of the*

HERBERT AND JANE DWIGHT WORKING GROUP
ON ISLAMISM AND THE INTERNATIONAL ORDER

Herbert and Jane Dwight
Stephen Bechtel Foundation
Lynde and Harry Bradley Foundation
Mr. and Mrs. Clayton W. Frye Jr.
Lakeside Foundation

CONTENTS

FOREWORD

FOR DECADES, THE THEMES of the Hoover Institution
have revolved around the broad concerns of political
and economic and individual freedom. The Cold War that
engaged and challenged our nation during the twentieth
century guided a good deal of Hoover's work, including its
archival accumulation and research studies. The steady output of work on the communist world offers durable testi-
monies to that time, and struggle. But there is no repose
from history's exertions, and no sooner had communism
left the stage of history than a huge challenge arose in the
broad lands of the Islamic world. A brief respite, and a me-
andering road, led from the fall of the Berlin Wall on 11/9
in 1989 to 9/11. Hoover's newly launched project, the Herbert and Jane Dwight Working Group on Islamism and the
International Order, is our contribution to a deeper understanding of the struggle in the Islamic world between order
and its nemesis, between Muslims keen to protect the rule
of reason and the gains of modernity, and those determined
to deny the Islamic world its place in the modern international order of states. The United States is deeply engaged,

and dangerously exposed, in the Islamic world, and we see our working group as part and parcel of the ongoing confrontation with the radical Islamists who have declared war on the states in their midst, on American power and interests, and on the very order of the international state system. The Islamists are doubtless a minority in the world of Islam. But they are a determined breed. Their world is the Islamic emirate, led by self-styled "emirs and mujahedeen in the path of God" and legitimized by the pursuit of the caliphate that collapsed with the end of the Ottoman Empire in 1924. These masters of terror and their foot soldiers have made it increasingly difficult to integrate the world of Islam into modernity. In the best of worlds, the entry of Muslims into modern culture and economics would have presented difficulties of no small consequence: the strictures on women, the legacy of humiliation and self-pity, the outdated educational systems, and an explosive demography that is forever at war with social and economic gains. But the borders these warriors of the faith have erected between Islam and "the other" are particularly forbidding. The lands of Islam were the lands of a crossroads civilization, trading routes and mixed populations. The Islamists have waged war, and a brutally effective one it has to be conceded, against that civilizational inheritance. The leap into the modern world economy as attained by China and India in recent years will be virtually impossible in a culture that feeds off belligerent self-pity, and endlessly calls for wars of faith.

The war of ideas with radical Islamism is inescapably central to this Hoover endeavor. The strategic context of this clash, the landscape of that Greater Middle East, is the other pillar. We face three layers of danger in the heartland of the Islamic world: states that have succumbed to the sway of terrorists in which state authority no longer exists (Afghanistan, Somalia, and Yemen), dictatorial regimes that suppress their people at home and pursue deadly weapons of mass destruction and adventurism abroad (Iraq under Saddam Hussein, the Iranian theocracy), and "enabler" regimes, such as the ones in Egypt and Saudi Arabia, which export their own problems with radical Islamism to other parts of the Islamic world and beyond. In this context, the task of reversing Islamist radicalism and of reforming and strengthening the state across the entire Muslim world—the Middle East, Africa, as well as South, Southeast, and Central Asia—is the greatest strategic challenge of the twenty-first century. The essential starting point is detailed knowledge of our enemy.

Thus, the working group will draw on the intellectual resources of Hoover and Stanford and on an array of scholars and practitioners from elsewhere in the United States from the Middle East and the broader world of Islam. The scholarship on contemporary Islam can now be read with discernment. A good deal of it, produced in the immediate aftermath of 9/11, was not particularly deep and did not stand the test of time and events. We, however, are in the favorable position of a "second generation" assessment of that Islamic material. Our scholars and experts can report, in a detailed, authoritative way, on Islam within the Arabian Peninsula, on trends within Egyptian Islam, on the struggle between the Kemalist secular tradition in Turkey and the new Islamists, particularly the fight for the loyalty of European Islam between these who accept the canon, and the discipline, of modernism and those who don't.

Arabs and Muslims need not be believers in American exceptionalism, but our hope is to engage them in this contest of ideas. We will not necessarily aim at producing primary scholarship, but such scholarship may materialize in that our participants are researchers who know their subjects intimately. We see our critical output as essays accessible to a broader audience, primers about matters that require explication, op-eds, writings that will become part of the public debate, and short, engaging books that can illuminate the choices and the struggles in modern Islam.

We see this endeavor as a faithful reflection of the values that animate a decent, moderate society. We know the travails of modern Islam, and this working group will be unsparing in depicting them. But we also know that the battle for modern Islam is not yet lost, that there are brave men and women fighting to retrieve their faith from the extremists. Some of our participants will themselves be intellectuals and public figures who have stood up to the pressure. The working group will be unapologetic about America's role in the Muslim world. A power that laid to waste religious tyranny in Afghanistan and despotism in Iraq, that came to the rescue of the Muslims in the Balkans when they appeared all but doomed, has given much to those burdened populations. We haven't always understood Islam and Muslims— hence this inquiry. But it a given of the working group that the pursuit of modernity and human welfare, and of the rule of law and reason, in Islamic lands is the common ground between America and contemporary Islam.

"WHAT WE HAVE HERE is a failure to communicate." This famous line from an old movie—*Cool Hand Luke*—poses an array of prior questions. Is radical Islamism a religious thing? An Arab thing? A clash of cultures? Communication for what and with whom? Or as put later in the film, maybe "some people you just can't reach."

There is no better guide through this thicket than John Hughes: a wise and tough old-school foreign correspondent who became a major newspaper editor, owner of his own chain of papers, Ronald Reagan's pick to direct the United States Information Agency and Voice of America, George Shultz's State Department spokesman and public affairs chief, chairman of a presidential task force on international broadcasting, and now professor of international communication at Brigham Young University. From the heights of such unparalleled career experience John Hughes explains the successes of America's Cold War informational-cultural policies and institutions and then describes the sickening dismantling of them in the post–Cold War decade.

Indonesia, the world's most populous Muslim country, was the nation where John Hughes won his Pulitzer Prize for international reporting on the communist attempt to overthrow the regime of President Sukarno in 1965—"The year of living dangerously." Hughes vividly describes the terror and political machinations of that era when the violent revolutionary cadres of an international atheistic ideology threw themselves at nationalistic autocracies whose claim on outside support rested mainly on their anticommunism. Only recently have some commentators concluded that such confrontations so damaged the values and aspirations of ordinary people that radical Islamism was thereby offered fertile soil in which to grow and begin to impose its own special formula for oppression.

Yet, this did not happen in Indonesia. Muslim faith and practice across that vast archipelago flourished, quietly resistant to the cry of fiery voices from radical mosques. In recent years Islamic Indonesia has only seemed to improve its commitment to good national governance and responsible international citizenship.

The distinguished anthropologist, the late Clifford Geertz, after long observation in Indonesia, pointed to that people's historic and cultural propensity to accept and blend with many diverse traditions while maintaining an easy relation to scriptural doctrine.

John Hughes' unique ability to bridge the issues of international communication to the remarkable case of Indonesia makes this a book of exceptional significance today. His conclusions and recommendations for American policy changes are required reading for all foreign affairs and national security decision-makers.

FOUAD AJAMI
Senior Fellow, Hoover Institution
Cochairman, Herbert and Jane Dwight Working
Group on Islamism and the International Order

CHARLES HILL
Senior Fellow, Hoover Institution
Cochairman, Herbert and Jane Dwight Working
Group on Islamism and the International Order

The Rise and Fall of USIA

*"America is a shining city upon a hill whose beacon light
guides freedom-loving people everywhere."*

RONALD REAGAN

A MERICA AND ITS ALLIES have been challenged in
contemporary times by three dangerous "isms." Fascism was bred and defeated in Europe. Communism, now
a pale and shrinking force, was nurtured in the Soviet
Union but confronted on a global platform. Islamism, or
Islamic extremism, which exploded on American soil on
September 11, 2001, is rooted in the Arab lands of the Middle East and has developed a clientele worldwide.

Each of these three pernicious ideologies has necessarily
been confronted by military force. Most recently, the
United States has found it necessary to wage a war on terrorism against Islamist extremists. The United States must
remain engaged in this conflict as long as the practitioners

of Islamic extremism continue to conduct a murderous jihad against Americans in particular, but many other nationalities as well.

America has mobilized much manpower and materiel to protect its homeland and carry the fight to the enemy's remote lairs and hiding places. But it is the war of words and ideas that will ultimately determine whether moderate Islam, with which the United States has no quarrel, will prevail over Islamic extremism, whose perversion of Islamic faith is the problem.

It is a contest in which the extremists are proving adept. From the remote terrain of the Afghanistan-Pakistan border they project their anti-American propaganda on Al Jazeera, which is then picked up by CNN and other television networks and broadcast worldwide. Their production of material for television has become increasingly sophisticated. They have become adept at using the Internet to spread their doctrine. The now-famous letter from Osama bin Laden's closest lieutenant, Ayman Al Zawahiri to Al Qaeda's number one operative in Iraq, Abu Musab Al Zarqawi, who is now dead, made the strategy clear: "More than half the battle is taking place on the battlefield of the media. We are in a media race . . . for hearts and minds."[1]

Public diplomacy is the critical U.S. weapon in this battle, rebutting falsehoods, and projecting a truthful picture and explanation of American policies, culture, and freedoms. Traditional diplomacy is usually government-to-government, conducted by diplomats in confidence and behind closed doors. Public diplomacy is open and is usually conducted through media in an attempt to persuade mass audiences, or elites who are influential with mass audiences.

Probably the best-known American instrument of public diplomacy has been the Voice of America (VOA), broadcasting by shortwave radio around the world. Launched in 1942, its first broadcasts were in German, its first director was John Houseman, its first message: "The news may be good or bad. We shall tell you the truth." So it has over the years, while adapting itself to FM and medium-wave radio, television, the Internet, and new kinds of communication. Today it broadcasts in 45 languages to 134 million people.

After World War II, and with the advent of the Cold War, President Eisenhower in 1953 authorized a new entity, the United States Information Agency (USIA). It embraced various existing government information units (with the exception of educational and cultural exchanges, which remained under the State Department) and built a powerful organization to counter Soviet propaganda and to "tell America's story to the world."

The USIA, with VOA operating under its aegis, mounted a formidable, multifaceted public diplomacy operation to implement its mission. It launched a daily wireless file to every American embassy that clarified policy and contained information diplomats could use in engagement with local opinion-makers. It produced a serious publication, *Problems of Communism,* which reached scholars around the world.

From its printing plants in Manila and Mexico City came a succession of free colorful magazines about America in various languages. A Russian-language edition became so popular in Moscow that Soviet officials clamped down on it; they sent bundles back to the United States, claiming nobody wanted to read it. That made it a hot black market item for which ordinary Russians paid the equivalent of several dollars a copy.

On the cultural front, the USIA, in tandem with the State Department, sent dance and musical groups—musicians like Dizzy Gillespie and Benny Goodman—around the world, including tours to Russia and its satellite nations in Eastern Europe whenever feasible. Among various educational and exchange programs to Africa and the Middle East, the USIA promoted a notable 1953 colloquium featuring Islamic and American scholars at Princeton.

One of the most effective public diplomacy programs brought government officials and politicians, journalists and writers, and artists and opinion-makers from other countries for stays of varying length to observe America in all its strengths and weaknesses. USIA programmers targeted young politicians later to become leaders in their own countries. Such individuals included Anwar Sadat, Margaret Thatcher, Tony Blair, Hamid Karzai, and Gerhard Schröder. It is tempting to ponder what impact, if any, such a visit to the United States in earlier days might have made upon Saddam Hussein.

Operating abroad as the United States Information Service (USIS), the USIA screened and distributed American movies, as well as documentaries it commissioned itself, from leading American moviemakers. Wherever it could, it opened U.S. libraries and reading rooms in major foreign cities. As a foreign correspondent in Africa and Asia, I found it moving to see these libraries crammed with students doing their homework and taking advantage of the large collections of American books, newspapers, and films.

The USIA also promoted big-ticket items like exhibits of American art and innovative pavilions displaying American products at international fairs. The famous "kitchen debate" between Richard Nixon and Nikita Khrushchev took place in 1959 at an American fair in Moscow. Almost three million Russians visited the American exhibits.

Role of the Radios

Meanwhile, the VOA broadcast straight news bulletins around the clock in different languages to countries all over the world despite Soviet attempts to jam the signal. By law, the VOA was precluded from directing its programs internally, to an American audience. But Americans could pick them up on a shortwave radio. James (Scotty) Reston, the *New York Times* columnist, did just that, tuning in the VOA's English language broadcast each evening. He told me that it was his favorite newscast.[2] In addition to news there was "back-of-the-book" programming, which included debates and discussions and features on American life and culture. Country music was a hit in many lands, but an enormous audience tuned in to VOA jazz programs. They were introduced with a recognizable "Yankee Doodle

Dandy" jingle and hosted by an eccentric but knowledgeable jazz buff, Willis Conover, who became a legend behind the Iron Curtain. When he was allowed to visit Poland, a crowd reputedly of thousands turned out to welcome him at the Warsaw airport.

Another intriguing program VOA developed was "Special English," designed to teach English to foreign listeners. The program was written in a reduced English vocabulary, and narrated substantially slower than other VOA programs. When years later I visited China, I was fascinated to hear bellboys and other staff in my hotel learning English from the VOA.

While VOA broadcast world news to a world audience, Radio Free Europe and Radio Liberty were broadcasting to East Europe and Russia, respectively. The mission of these radio networks was narrower. Staffed by many expatriates from their targeted countries, they were designed to gather factual information about what was happening in those countries and broadcast it back to peoples behind the Iron Curtain where censorship would otherwise bar them from hearing it. They were to be the radio stations that citizens would hear in those countries if they were free.

Originally financed by the Central Intelligence Agency (CIA), that link was later broken and they became financed by congressional budget and operated by radio professionals, responsible to a new oversight entity, the Board for International Broadcasting.

The evidence is overwhelming that the work of these radio stations and the VOA, broadcasting to captive peo-

ples, played a significant role in keeping the concept of freedom alive behind the Iron Curtain. When Lech Walesa was
asked, after the events of 1989, if Radio Free Europe had
played a role in the rebirth of freedom, he replied: "Would
there be earth without the sun?"[3] Czechoslovakia's Vaclev
Havel made his statement symbolically. The day he took
office as his country's new president he went to the offices
of Voice of America and said simply: "Thank you."[4]

When I became director of the VOA during the Reagan
administration, I was moved to receive messages, sometimes by circuitous routes, from listeners in Eastern Europe
and the Soviet Union. Some would tell of creeping out into
the birch forests in winter snow to listen to the VOA on a
hidden shortwave radio. Wrote one man: "Your broadcasts
from Voice of America keep the flame of liberty burning in
our breasts."

During the political upheaval in the Soviet Union, VOA
reporters were trapped on the barricades of the Russian parliament. Using their cellular phones they gave the world the
first news of the depth of the Russian resistance. Their reports went straight to the Moscow bureau of the VOA,
which beamed them live to the VOA headquarters in Washington, which then broadcast them almost instantly back to
millions of listeners across the Soviet Union, buoying their
spirits and stiffening their resolve.

There was the extraordinary image of Boris Yeltsin rush-
ing a crucial speech to an aide, who faxed it to America with
the words: "The Russian government has no ways to address the people. All radio stations here are under control.

Following is Yeltsin's address to the army. Submit it to USIA. Broadcast it over the country. Maybe 'Voice of America.' Do it. Urgent."[5] And finally, another extraordinary image of the isolated Gorbachev, searching for word of his and his country's future by turning, as his countrymen long had, to Radio Liberty and the Voice of America.

With the end of the Cold War, it became logical to examine the continuing role of the government radio stations. In April of 1991, President George Bush announced an independent, bipartisan presidential task force to consider the facts and report back to him in six months. Chaired by me, it contained such prominent Americans as David Abshire, president of the Center for Strategic and International Studies; Richard Allen, assistant to the president for national security affairs in the Reagan administration; Stuart Eizenstat, a special White House adviser in the Carter administration; writer Peggy Noonan; syndicated columnist Ben Wattenberg; Abbott Washburn, a former deputy director of USIA; Richard Fairbanks, former special negotiator for the Middle East peace process; Rozanne Ridgway, president of the Atlantic Council; Viviane Warren, a prominent figure in public broadcasting; and Rita Clements, a former first lady of Texas.

The task force took testimony from many experts, pored over several hundred documents and reports, traveled to London to examine BBC international radio programming and to Munich to visit with Radio Free Europe and Radio Liberty executives, and met with senior officials from a number of Eastern European countries.

The group quickly came to the view that the radio services, which had played such an important role in the Cold War, had a "crucial" role in the post–Cold War atmosphere. "Communist totalitarianism has been severely wounded but has not expired everywhere," they wrote in their final report. "No one knows what comes next. It is important that America continue to lead a peaceful global effort to promote democratic values, particularly in large parts of Asia and Cuba, the last redoubts of a pernicious ideology. In this task, the role of American international broadcasting is crucial."[6] The task force conceded that the "global contest of ideas" would likely move in some different directions in the years to come. It predicted that as the United States continued to promote democratic values, another important issue would surface, namely: "What kind of democracy?" The task force reminded readers of its report that "American-style democracy is not necessarily the same as European-style, or Scandinavian-style, or Japanese-style democracy. We should not dictate precise forms of democratic organization to the world. America itself is different; scholars call it 'American Exceptionalism.' . . . [W]hile far from perfect, under challenge in some respects, this way of life is seen as revolutionary and admirable by people all around the world, in the unfree states, in the emerging democracies, and in our sister democracies. . . . [M]ost Americans today properly feel that we have something useful to offer the world . . . it would be a shame if we did not offer what we have. Such a course is right morally, and right from a point of self-interest. Americans want a world that is user-friendly to our values."[7]

Conceding that Radio Free Europe and Radio Liberty might ultimately be phased out, the task force maintained that they should continue for some years in a somewhat modified role. Instead of operating as surrogate radio services to nations once under communist domination, they should offer alternative broadcasting to assist newly democratic nations to establish democratic institutions, particularly free and unfettered media.

The value of this proposal was made clear in Munich when a senior Czech official dealing with the media met with our task force. He explained that during the Cold War most Czech journalists had been communists used to writing and broadcasting under authoritarian diktat. When the Cold War came to an end, they had difficulty making the transition to a free press. At joint press conferences with American reporters, the Americans asked all the tough questions while the Czech reporters held back. Our Czech official told us that he summoned the Czech reporters to his office and said the Americans were making the reticent Czech reporters look bad. He urged them to be more questioning of authority. The next press conference was initially better. The Czechs and the Americans both pressed the Czech official conducting the conference. But after the conference was ended, the Czech reporters crowded into the official's office. Still steeped in their old ways of being instructed what to report, they said: "OK, we've done what you wanted. Now what do you want us to write?"

Insofar as the flagship VOA was concerned, the task force recommended substantially increased funding and expanding resources for more shortwave broadcasting as well as transmission with emerging technologies. The task force saw "an indefinite and expanding need" for the VOA to increase its coverage of Asia, Africa, the Middle East, and Latin America.

While change might have surged across Eastern and Central Europe and the then Soviet Union, the task force declared: "There remains a world that is fluid, and sometimes dangerous. The [first] Gulf war is a reminder of how conflicts can explode into international ones overnight. The Middle East remains riven with violence and extremism. . . . [T]he West is still seen as the Great Satan to some of the people of Islam."

Thus, the task force concluded: "This is no time to abandon or degrade America's great international broadcasting endeavor . . . this is the time to enhance, redirect and revitalize the mission . . . for now as ever, these unique tools of public diplomacy can serve our nation."[8]

If the task force enthused over the VOA and Radio Free Europe/Radio Liberty continuing to carry out their separate missions, it had questions about the effectiveness of Radio Marti and TV Marti, created in 1983 and 1989, respectively, to continue broadcasting to Cuba. Cuba under Fidel Castro had been cast as a captive and unfree nation by the U.S. government. The Marti radio and TV operations were thus supposed to mirror the early roles of Radio Free Europe and Radio Liberty—providing for Cubans the kind of information they would have had if living in a democracy. But the Castro regime went to extraordinary lengths to jam

11

Radio Marti and black out TV Marti. Over the years the size of the listening and viewing Cuban audience has continued to raise questions about the efficacy of the Marti operation. In 2010 a report to the U.S. Senate recommended subordinating the Marti operation under VOA.

Radio Free Asia

After the prodemocracy uprising in Beijing's Tiananmen Square, there was a movement in both houses of Congress to launch a new surrogate U.S. broadcasting service predominantly to China but also to other countries in Asia living under totalitarian regimes. "Surrogate," of course, meant that such broadcasting would be cast in the image of Radio Free Europe, attempting to offer the kind of internal news coverage that the populations of these countries would enjoy if they were free.

The State Department did not favor such a project, arguing that it would be harmful to U.S.-China relations. Surrogate radio for China would likely have an effect opposite to the one intended, said State in testimony before the task force. It would lead to less freedom for China because the Chinese government would "likely respond by increasing internal political repression."

State also pointed out that VOA was already broadcasting to China in Mandarin, Cantonese, Tibetan, and English and that China would likely respond to the "provocation of a surrogate service to China" by increased jamming of VOA's services. While mindful of State's viewpoint, the task force responded that the same arguments could have been made against Radio Free Europe and Radio Liberty when they started in 1949 and 1951, respectively, but these radios helped move the world toward freedom. Said the task force: "Both diplomacy and communication are needed, are necessary and are appreciated. But the history of the past few decades suggests that diplomacy helped keep the world safe, ideas helped make the world free."[9]

All of the task force's members agreed that VOA broadcasting into China had been of great value and should be strengthened.

The task force was split on the issue of a Radio Free Asia broadcasting to China and other unfree nations in Asia. The majority favored it; a minority was opposed, citing questions about cost and transmitter availability and urging instead strengthened VOA broadcasting to China, Vietnam, Cambodia, Laos, and North Korea.

However, even before the task force could present its findings on this issue to the president, there was a new development. In October of 1991, Congress passed a bill, introduced by Senator Joseph Biden, establishing a joint congressional/presidential commission. It was to "examine the feasibility, effect and implications" of instituting a radio broadcasting service to the People's Republic of China and other Communist countries in Asia in order "to promote the dissemination of ideas, with particular emphasis on developments within each of these nations."[10] The president appointed me as chairman and two other members of the commission. The Senate appointed two Republicans and two Democrats; the House of Representatives appointed two Republicans and two Democrats.

The commission sought testimony from experts political and technical in Washington, New York, Los Angeles, San Francisco, Boston, Munich, Honolulu, Seoul, Bangkok, Hong Kong, and Taiwan. It amassed volumes of detailed information on existing and possible transmitter sites. It acquired estimates of cost and staffing.

Without much hope of a constructive discussion, we sought permission from North Korea's representative at the United Nations (UN) for the commission to visit his country. I tried to keep my end of the telephone conversation polite. I can only describe the reaction from the other end of the line—during which the North Korean diplomat suggested an intriguing number of nongeographic destinations the commission could go to—as sulfurous.

The reaction from the Chinese was much more sophisticated but equally negative. Their ambassador in Washington informed me that our commission could not be recognized but its members could visit China as individual guests of the U.S. embassy in Beijing. During the visit commission members must refrain from any actions "incompatible with their status." They must refrain from any actions or remarks in the name of the commission. Individual members should abide by Chinese laws and regulations so that "nothing unpleasant" would occur. Requests for meetings with relevant departments would be made in advance through the U.S. embassy.[11]

Finally, one of the commission's members, Steven Mosher, director of the Asian Studies Center at the Claremont Institute in California, would "not be welcome."

We surmised that this had something to do with Mr. Mosher's writings on Chinese population control. The commission quickly caucused. It decided unanimously that even if we could have agreed—although unlikely—with the other requirements, we could not accept the blackballing of one of our members. The vote was unanimous and instant: either we all went, or none of us went. I replied to the Chinese ambassador accordingly.

In its report to Congress and the president the commission declared:

"The United States has a unique opportunity at this moment in history to assist the wave of democracy that already has touched such Asian lands as the Philippines, South Korea, and Taiwan.

The United States should do this because it is right.

The United States should do this because it is in its national interest."[12]

The commission recommended "home service" broadcasting to China, North Korea, Vietnam, Cambodia, and Burma (now Myanmar). It added Burma because, although not a Communist country, Burma's ruling dictatorship "is one of the most repressive in the world." It used the term "home service" as an alternative for "surrogate" to describe "broadcast information about events and developments within the country itself—that would be available if there were no government censorship, and no repressive control of media." In other words, it was drawing a distinction between VOA-type broadcasting and Radio Free Europe broadcasting.

Radio Free Asia went into business in 1996 and in time broadcast in nine Asian languages—Mandarin, Tibetan, Burmese, Vietnamese, Korean, Laotian, Khmer, Cantonese, and Uyghur.

Korean Airliner 007

During the darkest days of the Cold War, USIA was tasked to refute egregious examples of Soviet disinformation. These included clever forgeries of State Department and other official documents inventing bogus and damaging stories about U.S. activities. One fabricated story was that Americans were involved in an illegal Central American scheme to acquire children's body parts for wealthy American recipients. Another fabrication was a news dispatch reporting that the American embassy in New Delhi housed a giant computer which had collected personal information about every citizen of India. Yet another was that the United States had created the AIDS virus for use as a biological weapon.

One of the most embarrassing public diplomacy setbacks for the Soviet Union occurred in 1983 when Soviet fighter pilots shot down a South Korean airliner, flight 007, which had strayed briefly off course, over Soviet territory, on a trans-Pacific flight. Two hundred and sixty-nine passengers and crew, including an American congressman, were killed. I was serving as assistant secretary for public affairs and spokesman at the State Department at the time and was summoned early in the morning to join Secretary George Shultz and Undersecretary Lawrence Eagleburger in the secretary's office. They were in animated talk over early reports of the shoot-down. The Soviets were keeping silent—as they were to do for several days, after which they initially denied involvement. Our discussion revolved around what we knew and how we were to present our version of what had happened. Eagleburger, a man of great passions, declared angrily: "They shot it down and we know they did."

I caught a reference to "the tape."

"What tape?" I asked.

He disclosed that a top secret monitoring unit, outside the United States, had recorded the Soviet pilots' chatter as they locked on to the Korean airliner. "We have to play the tape," I said. "Can't do it," said Eagleburger. Another government was involved, and, even if that problem could be overcome, if we played the tape, the Russians would learn that we were monitoring their frequencies. They would change all of them and an intelligence advantage would be lost. There followed a robust exchange between Eagleburger and myself as we debated the pros and cons in front of Secretary Shultz. Eagleburger was a great man at a great moment. In the end, he agreed that the sensational political import of the tapes outweighed the loss of intelligence advantage. Within a day or so, we had the tape. We heard the Russian pilots communicating with their base, saying that they had sighted the airliner, seen its flashing lights, locked on, fired, and "destroyed" the "target."

USIA was called in to translate from the Russian, imprint English-language subtitles, and prepare it for presentation at a meeting of the UN Security Council. Huge monitoring screens were set up around the chamber. The world was stunned as U.S. ambassador to the UN Jeane Kirkpatrick played the dramatic tape in Russian, the words in English flashing across the screens. USIA, VOA, and the other government radios went on overtime, saturating the world's airwaves and media with the dramatic story. Nicholas Cull, a professor of public diplomacy at the University of Southern California, cited Izvestia's Alexander Shalnev as privately calling it "America's most devastating propaganda blow of the entire Cold War."[13] USIA officers in countries around the world made sure that the story was relayed to millions of readers, listeners, and viewers.

Innovative and inspiring as all the USIA and VOA programs were, much of the strength of U.S. public diplomacy lay in the talent of USIA public affairs officers stationed in the capitals and major cities of the world. Most were fluent in the languages of the countries they worked in. They were experienced practitioners of public diplomacy, well versed in the policies of their own nation, and adept at communicating and explaining them. They had generally, over time, developed extensive contacts in media and politics in the lands they served in. If a visiting American VIP was in town, they could generally introduce him, or her, to leading newspaper editors and TV directors or arrange dinners with officials and thought-leaders.

In the cities in which they were stationed, they ran American libraries and cultural centers, frequented by hundreds of students. They facilitated visits to the United States by prominent politicians, journalists, writers, and artists from the countries they were assigned to. They masterminded return visits to those countries by American musicians, dance groups, and other performers.

They were professional communicators with a passion for telling the American story. They were not hobbled by the bureaucracies of their embassies because they reported not to the State Department in Washington but to area directors of their own agency, USIA, who shared and understood the overall mission.

The Final Act

If USIA enjoyed its heyday during the Cold War, it ended that war, and its own existence, with a flourish.

When Ronald Reagan, who understood the power of communication, became president, he brought with him to Washington a number of friends who were members of his California "kitchen cabinet." Among them was a businessman and Hollywood aficionado called Charles Wick. While Wick and Reagan were good friends, their respective wives were even closer, having carpooled their children and socialized in the Los Angeles area. Every Christmas Eve, the Wicks and the Reagans enjoyed a private dinner together.

Reagan made Wick director of USIA. The skeptical Washington community pondered what skills Wick had for the job.

I did not know Charles Wick when he called me in Massachusetts. I had left the editorship of the *Christian Science Monitor* and was happily running a chain of small newspapers I owned on Cape Cod. "It's time for you to come and serve your country," Wick boomed. "Come down and let's talk." He wanted me to serve as associate director of USIA. I went to Washington on a reconnaissance. I was bemused when he said, "I don't know anything about journalism or anything about foreign affairs." But, he said, "I can make things happen." And he could.

As I found out when I began working for him, he could come up with a dozen new ideas in a few minutes. Seven or eight of them would be impossible. Wick would noisily berate anybody within hearing for their inability to capture his vision. Then he would break out into a grin and declare: "They were pretty lousy, weren't they?" But the two or three that would be really good, but that would be difficult, one would think, to implement in bureaucratic Washington, he would carry forward with great success. Wick could pick up the phone and call his friend, the president. He could call corporate chieftains and Hollywood stars and recruit them for his latest project—to appear in USIA films, or raise money for benefits, or go abroad as cultural ambassadors, or donate plane seats for exchange programs.

President Carter had changed the USIA brand name to USICA—the United States International Communication Agency. Agency personnel hated it. Some people overseas thought it had something to do with the CIA. Wick got Reagan to change it back to USIA, an immensely popular move with his staff.

Wick launched WORLDNET, linking USIA headquarters in Washington with U.S. embassies around the world, for live, interactive video discussions between foreign journalists and senior Washington officials.

I had an anxious moment when orchestrating one of them. The Washington guest in the studio was then secretary of state Alexander Haig. He was being interviewed live by Japanese correspondents in Tokyo. There had been a fair amount of reportage about bad blood between Secretary Haig and Defense Secretary Caspar Weinberger. With about 20 seconds left to go, a Japanese reporter asked Haig about it. "Nothing to it," responded Haig. "Why," he said, "Weinberger and I have breakfast together every week and there's nobody else there—except our food tasters." At that moment our line went dead, and I long wondered what the Japanese newsmen had made of Haig's intended humor.

Wick lobbied President Reagan to support new resources and major budget increases for USIA. The president came through. Wick got a new headquarters building for USIA. Wick launched "Project Truth," a sophisticated operation for countering Soviet disinformation.

When Poland feared Soviet military invasion, Wick raised half a million dollars from corporate chieftains and produced "Let Poland Be Poland," aired by satellite TV to some 184 million viewers around the world. Charlton Heston narrated. Frank Sinatra sang. Bob Hope and Orson Welles participated.

But as the Cold War, in which public diplomacy had clearly played a significant role, drew to a close, so too did the life of USIA as an independent agency. Congress, in its wisdom, sought ways to pare the budget, as did the new Clinton administration. Perhaps they thought that the U.S. was no longer confronted by unfriendly regimes or entities that wished it harm. As has proved to be the case, that was a dreadfully mistaken view.

The Demise of USIA

There was much Washington maneuvering in 1997 involving the foreign affairs agencies of the government and their future as Republican senator Jesse Helms sought to cut their cost and the Clinton administration similarly looked for efficiencies. On the Democrats' side, James Rubin, at the State Department, floated a plan which would integrate USIA, the Arms Control and Disarmament Agency, and AID (Agency for International Development) into the State Department. Rubin had been a staffer for Senator Joe Biden and press spokesman for Madeleine Albright when she was U.S. ambassador to the UN, and he had worked on the Clinton-Gore campaign. When Albright became secretary of state, Rubin became her assistant secretary for public affairs and department spokesman.

Although President Clinton protested there was no quid pro quo, Senator Helms met the Democrats' desire for passage of the Chemical Weapons Convention, and Albright offered up the folding of USIA favored by Senator Helms. A transitional period of two years was set for the fusion of USIA with State, and in 1999 USIA became extinct as such.

VOA was integrated into a new institution for U.S. government broadcasting, the Broadcasting Board of Governors, which already monitored Radio Free Europe, Radio Liberty, Radio and TV Marti, and Radio Free Asia.

If there was apprehension about the wisdom of collapsing USIA into the State Department, it has proved well justified. Many veteran public affairs officers elected to retire, taking their years of expertise with them. Others who made the transfer found themselves assigned to State Department regional bureaus, reporting not to practitioners of public diplomacy but to foreign service officers with little interest in, or patience with, public diplomacy. While foreign service officers were on fast tracks for promotion, the reassigned USIA officers were not. Overall, the USIA veterans found a prevalent State Department culture of disdain for public diplomacy. The budget for it was shredded.

In foreign posts, USIA officers were no longer running their own information centers and libraries, carrying out USIA policies and practices established in Washington, or reporting to their own USIA regional bureaus. Often they were inundated with regular embassy matters and bureaucratic rules and protocols unrelated to public diplomacy.

Meanwhile, a new post of undersecretary for public diplomacy and public affairs had been established at the State Department, but this officer did not manage public diplomacy funds or personnel that had been transferred to the regular State Department regional bureaus. Nor did any incumbent in this position have the status and heft that an agency director, namely director of USIA, had had in previous administrations. Small wonder that appointees to this new position did not linger long.

The Shock of 9/11

With the terrorist attack on the United States of September 2001, America was suddenly confronted by the new and dangerous ideology of Islamic extremism. U.S. public diplomacy was ill prepared to confront it, with inadequate resources, poor leadership, and organizational ineffectiveness.

As the initial response revolved around military defense and reaction, various entities and individuals marshaled the case for the renaissance of public diplomacy. It was sorely needed. The official 9/11 commission reported that after strong initial international support for the United States immediately following the initial terrorist attacks in New York and Washington, by 2003 "the bottom had fallen out of support for America in most of the Muslim world." Favorable ratings for the United States had fallen from 61 percent to 15 percent in Indonesia and from 71 percent to 38 percent among Muslims in Nigeria.

The commission reasoned that the small numbers of Muslims committed to Osama bin Laden were "impervious to persuasion." But "it is among the large majority of Arabs and Muslims that we must encourage reform, freedom, democracy, and opportunity, even though our own promotion of these messages is limited in its effectiveness simply because we are its carriers." The commission argued that "Muslims themselves will have to reflect upon such basic issues as the concept of jihad, the position of women, and the place of non-Muslim minorities. The United States can promote moderation, but cannot ensure its ascendancy. Only Muslims can do this."[14]

The Council on Foreign Relations, in a fast reaction, warned within a month of the 9/11 attack that "the federal bureaucracy is not configured to handle the demands of a major public diplomacy campaign. Public diplomacy is a low bureaucratic priority, as reflected by . . . the meager resources normally allocated to it."[15]

An independent task force the Council set up for deeper investigation found little improvement by 2003. It concluded: "The U.S. has significantly underperformed in its efforts to capture the hearts and minds of foreign publics. The marginalization of public diplomacy has left a legacy of underfunded and uncoordinated efforts. Lack of political will and the absence of an overall strategy has rendered past public diplomacy programs virtually impotent in today's crowded communications world. While sound public diplomacy is not a silver bullet for America's image problem, making it a serious composite of the foreign policymaking process is a vital step toward ensuring the nation's security."[16]

Specific task force recommendations urged training of U.S. ambassadors and diplomats in public diplomacy techniques; recruitment of "young and moderate Arabs and Muslims, mullahs, journalists and talk-show personalities" to criticize flaws within their own regimes; U.S. cultivation of foreign journalists; less "push-down" in communicating U.S. policies and more listening; better use of new digital technologies; more cultural and educational exchanges; more congressional support for public diplomacy.

There followed a steady stream of reports from institutions worried about the government's run-down public diplomacy apparatus and recommending change.

Congress instructed the State Department to set up an advisory group for the Arab and Muslim world to recommend new public diplomacy approaches. Chaired by Edward Djerjian, a former diplomat and White House press aide, it urged "an immediate end to the absurd and dangerous underfunding of public diplomacy in time of peril" and warned starkly: "If America does not define itself, the extremists will do it for us."[17]

The Djerjian report believed that the State Department should remain the government's lead public diplomacy agency but should be overseen by a cabinet-level special counselor for public diplomacy in the White House. Like almost all other reports, it recommended more money and staff for public diplomacy, more exchanges and scholarships, more use of the Internet and new technology. It suggested creating an independent Corporation for Public Diplomacy for private and nonprofit broadcasting and a program to translate thousands of the best American books in local languages for placement in libraries and universities and "American Corners" overseas.

As USIS centers and libraries abroad had become targets for rioters, they had been downsized and placed as "American Corners" in local libraries or more secure buildings. In my own experience in Africa and Asia, I had been saddened to see how remote and barricaded they had often become. It took a hardy visitor to produce acceptable identification, then negotiate bulletproof vestibules, frisking machines, armed guards, and surrender any packages or backpacks before gaining entry, sometimes in high-rise buildings with minimum sign-posting of their presence.

The U.S. government's own independent watchdog agency, the Government Accountability Office, raised major questions about public diplomacy performance in a series of reports over the years.

In 2005: "Prior reports by GAO and a number of other groups suggest that U.S. public diplomacy efforts over the past several years have generally not been successful. . . . The government does not yet have a national communication strategy."[18]

In 2006: "State has initiated three public diplomacy activities focused on the Muslim world—a media campaign, a youth-oriented magazine, and a group of youth-focused exchange programs—but these have been largely terminated or suspended."[19]

And: "30 percent of language-designated public diplomacy positions in the Muslim world were filled without the requisite language skills."

In 2007: "Key problems . . . include a general lack of strategic planning, inadequate coordination, and problems measuring performance and results. Beginning in 2003 we reported that the government lacked an interagency communications strategy. Four years later, a strategy still has not been released."[20]

In 2009: "Since the September 11, 2001, terrorist attacks, the U.S. government has spent at least $10 billion on communication efforts. . . . However negative views towards the U.S. persist."[21]

The GAO (Government Accounting Office) was concerned about lack of coordination between the State Department and the Pentagon on public diplomacy.

It was concerned about leadership at the State Department. "The position of Under-Secretary for Public Diplomacy and Public Affairs has been vacant about 40 per cent of the time since 2001."

It was concerned about staff shortages in public diplomacy positions. The U.S. embassy in Nigeria, with 800 employees, had only three senior officers and public affairs were handled entirely by first-tour junior officers.

It was concerned about language capability. Twenty-five percent of public diplomacy officers in language-designated positions did not meet the language requirements. In Arabic language posts, 36 percent of the public diplomacy positions were filled by staff unable to speak Arabic at the designated level.

There is no question that the establishment of the position of undersecretary for public diplomacy and public affairs at the State Department without status and without direct control of public diplomacy officers and budget was highly questionable. To leave the position unfilled for substantial periods of time was incomprehensible.

First appointee to this position was Charlotte Beers, an advertising executive, who left after criticism of the techniques she applied. Next was Margaret Tutwiler, a well-respected former media expert in government, who left soon for a position in corporate life.

Then, with high expectation from many of us, came Karen Hughes, President Bush's much-valued former media adviser. I did not think Hughes would labor long under the frustrations of the role. But I had hope that her influence with the president would have enabled her to make to him the recommendation I believed necessary, namely to scrap the ill-conceived and poorly performing structure of the day and restore USIA to an independent role. If that were not politically feasible, then the old USIA's functions and budget and personnel should have been replicated, with considerable autonomy, under the State Department's mantle.

Hughes elected not to make that recommendation. She did some traveling to Muslim countries. She talked to Muslim women. She got some additional exchange programs under way. But within the confines of the department, she was only able to shift chairs around on deck rather than launch a new ship. Either the frustrations of the system, or the call of family in Texas, led her as well to move on.

Then came James Glassman, a media professional who foresaw the need for a more ambitious embrace of new Internet and other technology in communicating around the world. But Glassman came at the end of President Bush's term in office and was obligated to resign after less than a year.

During the presidential election campaign of 2008, both Senator John McCain and Senator Barack Obama pledged support of public diplomacy.

McCain said he thought the Clinton administration and Congress had made a mistake in abolishing USIA and moving its public diplomacy functions to the State Department. The Senator went on: "This amounted to unilateral disarmament in the war of ideas." He vowed, if elected, to work with Congress to create a new independent agency with the sole purpose of getting America's message to the world. This, he believed, was a "critical element in combating Islamic extremism and restoring the image of our country abroad."[22] Hillary Clinton testified at her confirmation hearing as President Obama's secretary of state that Obama would launch a "coordinated, multi-agency program of public diplomacy," but she did not foresee a return of the independent USIA. "It is more practical at this time," she said, to "improve the functioning of public diplomacy in the [State] department."[23]

Secretary Clinton filled the undersecretary of public diplomacy and public affairs slot with Judith McHale, a former television executive.

Radios and TV

If the integration of USIA's remnants into the State Department was dysfunctional, the transfer of the government's radio and TV operations to the direction of the Broadcasting Board of Governors (BBG), an independent federal agency, has not been without challenges. Though the broadcasters have been freed of traditional government bureaucracy, they have encountered a different set of controls and policy input from the independent but government-funded agency.

The BBG oversees all nonmilitary U.S. public diplomacy broadcasting. It is supposed to consist of nine members—four Republicans and four Democrats chosen by the president and confirmed by the Senate and the current secretary of state ex officio. But members from both left- and right-wing political persuasions have been accused of trying to exert political pressure at times, and the secretary of state has rarely attended its sessions. In 2009, it was down to four members, barely enough for a quorum with the undersecretary for public diplomacy and public affairs sitting in for the secretary of state.

At times the BBG has exhibited high energy, as for example when it included successful commercial broadcasters such as Democrat Norm Pattiz. A billionaire entrepreneur, he pressed for new services to the Muslim world such as Radio Sawa, an Arabic-language service heavy on popular music, Radio Farda, a similar station beamed at Iran, and Alhurra, an Arabic-language TV station. A strong supporter of government broadcasting has been former senator Joseph Biden, who championed Radio Farda. When the senator became vice president, his Senate seat was taken by Edward Kaufman, a former senior aide, who had held one of the Democratic seats on the Broadcasting Board of Governors. At a congressional hearing, Senator Kaufman termed the role of broadcasting to war zones like Afghanistan and Iraq "particularly critical" in winning hearts and minds. In many places in the world, he said, "if it wasn't for U.S. and international broadcasting the people would never hear what any of our public officials have to say on absolutely anything."[24]

But the BBG has imposed budget and programming decisions that have roused the ire of broadcasters in its various divisions. In 2008 its employees rated the board the worst ever for good management, placing it at the very bottom of federal agencies.

VOA has long been the flagship of U.S. government broadcasting, its brand name widely recognized throughout the world and its journalists proud of their reputation for producing quality international news. VOA has itself been torn at times between its charter obligation to "serve as a consistently reliable and authoritative source of news" that will be "accurate, objective, and comprehensive," and its other charter obligation "to present the policies of the United States clearly and effectively."[25] This apparent dichotomy of mission has at times set it apart from other government radios with the "surrogate" mission of broadcasters like Radio Free Europe, Radio Liberty, and Radio Free Asia, to unfree nations, and latterly the new commercial-style broadcasting to the Muslim world.

As USIA officers being integrated into the State Department in 1999 had to deal with a different culture long in history, so is there a longstanding VOA culture which has sometimes set VOA apart from the other, newer, government radios.

VOA employees have smarted under BBG decisions to cease or cut back programming in some of their 45 languages to 134 million listeners in order to fund new programs to the Muslim world. They found the cutback in English-language broadcasting particularly grievous.

All U.S. government broadcasters have had to adapt to the new technologies for communicating with target audiences.

They have had to face the reality of new competition from other international broadcasters like China and Russia and France and Germany, as well as a competing slew of radio and TV broadcasting from commercial Arab broadcasters, particularly Al Jazeera and Al Arabiya. When President Obama made the first broadcast in his presidency to the Arab world, he chose not the U.S. government's Alhurra TV station but the Saudi-owned Al Arabiya.

There is even competition and overlap from other government departments. The Pentagon has large funds for "strategic communication," which sometimes involves radio broadcasting. Even the State Department set up a program in 2009 to spend up to $150 million on local FM radio stations and cellphone service in Afghanistan and Pakistan to refute militant Taliban propaganda.

Meanwhile the U.S. government broadcasting family's own lineup is no longer clearly delineated by VOA, Radio Free Europe, and Radio Liberty but splintered by the additions of Radio Free Asia, Radio Farda in Persian, Radio Sawa in Arabic, Radio Free Iraq, Radio Azadi and Radio Ashna, and Alhurra.

The traditional rival for U.S. government broadcasters throughout the world is the BBC, which is now particularly competitive with radio and TV broadcasting to the Muslim world. Congressional and other critics of VOA sometimes hold up the BBC as an example, querying why the British broadcaster can sometimes claim more credibility with foreign listeners than the VOA.

While the BBC is funded by the British government with taxpayers' money, it protests vehemently that it is independent and does not echo the views of the British government. Its independent prospective has sometimes angered the British government, for example with the BBC's coverage of the Falklands war and reporting on affairs in Northern Ireland.

In response to its sometime critics, the VOA points to its bifurcated charter requirement of producing objective, authoritative news while simultaneously projecting government policy, a balancing act which the BBC avoids.

Two of the weakest BBG charges are Radio and TV Marti, broadcasting to Cuba, and Alhurra TV, broadcasting to Muslim countries.

In a 2009 assessment of Marti problems, the GAO reported poor management communication, low employee morale, and allegations of fraud and abuse since 1999 in the Miami-based operation.[26]

Despite expenditure of more than $500 million over two decades and annual costs of about $34 million, only 2 percent of respondents in Cuba surveyed by telephone reported having listened to Radio Marti or viewed TV Marti.

Alhurra TV has had a difficult history since its inception in 2004. Two years later the GAO accused it of poor management and weak performance. Its journalistic quality was questioned and its top management faulted for its inability to speak Arabic. After it was again criticized for covering a Holocaust denial conference in Tehran, and airing an hour-long speech by Hezbollah chief Hassan Nasrallah, it was the subject of congressional hearings and pressure. In 2008 it came under extensive criticism from media watchdog ProPublica, and CBS's *60 Minutes* for alleged anti-United States content. Its Baghdad bureau was charged with a pro-Iranian bias. A 2008 University of Southern California study commissioned by the BBG found that Alhurra's broadcasts to the Middle East failed to meet journalistic standards and were seen by few viewers.[27]

The BBG said it benefited from the critical findings but cited other views that Alhurra had put in place "more vigorous policies, procedures, training, and tools for transparency in order to preserve its credibility." It claimed Alhurra was "drawing the largest audience U.S. international broadcasting has ever attracted in the Middle East" and its stature and audience would grow.[28]

PART
II

Indonesia: Where Democracy and Islam Coexist

"Democracy is the worst form of government except all others."

WINSTON CHURCHILL

W HEN I WAS A FOREIGN CORRESPONDENT visiting Indonesia years ago, I would arrive in Jakarta, take an ancient taxi or *betjak* (pedicab), sprinkle my visiting cards around at the homes of generals, cabinet ministers, and old friends I wanted to see, then go back to my hotel and wait. There was no point in trying to reach these sources at their offices. In part, it was because Indonesia at that time was so poverty-wracked that they were all moonlighting at other jobs to make ends meet. In part, it was because in Indonesia's easygoing culture, they had their own way of making contact.

In time, the invitations would trickle back, sometimes circuitously: Drop in for Sunday breakfast with general so-and-so; maybe afternoon tea with the foreign minister; maybe a late-night têtc-à-têtc with someone who did not want to be seen with an American journalist.

All this was immensely frustrating to any lone American hustle-and-bustle businessman, flying in, expecting instant appointments, trying to close deals overnight before heading off to the next Asian country. But it was the Indonesian way, and in it there is perhaps a lesson worth pondering as we observe Indonesia today: the largest Islamic, but non-Arab, country in the world, with a population of more than 202 million. After many years of trial and turbulence, it is stable and more prosperous. Though there is still poverty and hardship in the countryside, Jakarta is now a capital of fine hotels, tall office blocks, and broad highways. Indonesia is comfortably meshing its devout but moderate brand of Islam with newfound democracy. It is, moreover, successfully fending off intermittent Islamist extremist attempts to disrupt its stability.

It was not ever thus. Indonesia had to survive almost 20 years of poor government, and a brush with communism, under one dictator, Sukarno (who like many Indonesians used only one name), and another 30 years of corrupt government under his successor, Suharto, before emerging from political darkness into light. It is perhaps this tortured history that helps make Indonesia sturdier today in defense of democracy and explains its disinclination to embrace extremism.

After colonization by the Dutch, and Japanese occupation during World War II, Indonesia seized its independence in 1945. It was a potentially rich country, with oil, a lot of timber, minerals, and metals. Much of its underground treasure had not been exploited. Often it was remote, in outlandish parts of Sumatra, or in the inaccessible wilds of Kalimantan. Its extraction would require roads, railways, machinery, and massive infusions of development capital, which the new government did not have readily at hand.

Sukarno, the first leader after independence, did little to improve the economic welfare of his people. But he did weld an array of islands flung in an arc across three thousand miles of ocean, stretching from Malaysia to Australia, into a single nation under one language. He became revered as the father of the nation, reveling in grandiose titles like Great Leader of the Revolution and Mouthpiece of the Indonesian People. To his countrymen he gave some of those intangibles particularly precious to peoples emerging from foreign rule: a sense of national identity and importance, racial pride, and the end of inequality and second-class citizenship.

He was a spellbinding entertainer. I saw him work his magic on a number of occasions. In a covered stadium packed with thousands, there would be a warm-up with political cheerleaders coaching various sections of the audience with slogan-shouting, cheering, and singing. Then faintly, from a distance, would come the sound of sirens from the approaching presidential convoy. The sirens would scream nearer and nearer, coming to a shrieking halt outside the stadium's main entrance. President Sukarno would emerge from his black limousine and stroll through an avenue of pretty girls, specially chosen and in national costume, who would strew a carpet of rose petals in front of him as he walked.

Inside the stadium, aides and bodyguards at his heels, he would take his place in a special reserved area about halfway up one side of the banked arena. Before him on a table would be his favorite brand of American cigarettes, a plate or two of cookies and sweet cakes, and always three glasses of liquid: reputedly tea, a soft drink, and perhaps a medicinal mixture, each covered with silver lids. High in the eaves would be elite presidential guards, their eyes darting suspiciously over the assembled throng.

There would be some preliminary speakers, in whom the president would indicate interest—or disdainful disinterest—as the mood took him. Then would come the moment for Sukarno himself to speak. Down the stairs he would pad to a dais on the floor of the arena, a stocky little man in a well-cut uniform gilded with medals and decorations, and always with a traditional black *pitji,* or Indonesian hat, on his head.

With a roar, the thousands would surge to their feet. The bright revolutionary banners floating from the walls would flutter a little in the sudden breeze. The air, it almost seemed, would crackle a little with the electric excitement.

Unsmiling, impassive, Sukarno would nod his head across the banked thousands, turning from one side of the arena to the other. For a few moments he would stand before the cluster of microphones on the dais, then flick a couple of them to make sure they were working. When he raised one finger briefly, perfunctorily, the crowd would instantly become silent.

He would begin to speak. Slowly at first, in a hoarse, caressing, mesmeric whisper. Then faster. And louder. And louder and faster still, until he had the crowd in an ecstatic fervor. Sometimes he would take them on flights of mystic fancy, as with words like: "How great is God, who gave that sense of struggle to me, when I as a youth, physically sitting on a grass mat under the flickering rays of a rushlight, conducted a mental dialogue in the metaphysical world with the great strugglers of many nations, with the thinkers of all nations who steered the course of history."

But then seconds later he would thunder and roll his eyes with: "I am a dynamic man. I don't like tranquility, which is frozen and dead, I don't like sluggishness. What I like is dynamism, vitality, militancy, activity, a revolutionary spirit. I prefer the painting of an ocean with boisterous waves, rather than a painting of rice fields full of calmness and tranquility. If it is a painting of rice fields, I would choose one where the paddy sways and the wind blows. If I am to choose a portrait, I choose one with fire, power, vitality."

If Sukarno seemed to project electricity in the air, he actually had a preoccupation with it. When he was still relatively cordial towards Americans, a political officer from the U.S. embassy sat next to him one night at dinner. She noticed that Sukarno shrugged off his shoes. Making conversation, she remarked upon this and asked him if he had had a hard day. "No," he replied with all seriousness, "it is to let the electricity out of my body."

Long after his reputation began to tarnish, Indonesians of the older generation still spoke with affection for him, waving aside his misdeeds like minor peccadilloes of an emperor too grand to do serious wrong.

Thus, when he argued that Western-style liberal democracy had failed in Indonesia and thrust it aside for his own "guided democracy," the country concurred. When he canceled further elections and assumed dictatorial powers, Indonesians sat submissively by. Only those political parties and groupings existed that had his nod of endorsement. Politicians, journalists, and others who incurred his disapproval disappeared from view. It was not his fashion to execute them. They languished in jails or exile. Sometimes, after repentance, they were brought back to positions of minor authority.

The country was run by presidential and prime ministerial fiat, and Sukarno was both president and prime minister. He lived in awesome splendor, with resplendent uniforms, grand palaces, expensive cars, and usually beautiful women on his arm. On borrowed money he built grandiose monuments in Jakarta, and played host to expensive conferences of delegates from "New Emerging Forces," or NEFOs, as he called them. He told his people that Jakarta and Beijing (because he had formed an alliance with China) now ranked with Washington and Moscow as the capitals that decided the world's destiny. No longer could Indonesia be called, as it once was by a Dutch colonial official, a "coolie among nations."

To enhance Indonesia's prestige, Sukarno squandered on guns and other military materiel. He spent millions of dollars on a navy from the Soviet Union, including an aging cruiser the Soviets were happy to unload. A high Indonesian official present at the bargaining between Khrushchev and Sukarno in Moscow told me that when Sukarno expressed interest in the warship, Khrushchev set a highly inflated price on it. Sukarno snapped it up. Khrushchev, according to the story, could barely hide his astonishment.

The cruiser rusted off Indonesia's Surabaya naval base, rarely putting to sea. It displayed only one side to public view. The story was that that was the only side regularly re-painted. The other, rusty, side was never displayed to eyes on shore.

As Sukarno squandered the country's wealth on such unproductive baubles, the economy deteriorated. Cotton mills began to stand idle. The rice harvest was no longer sufficient to feed the people and rice had to be imported.

It is difficult to assess accurately the stage at which Sukarno's magic began to fade—when he began, as his Japanese wife put it in a remarkably frank interview later, to lose touch with the people. Two factors contributed to the change in mood. One was the development of a new urbanized class, which had rising expectations that were not being fulfilled. The other was the slowly dawning suspicion that much of Sukarno's posturing, play-acting, and spending on prestige projects was more for the aggrandizement of Sukarno than for that of the Indonesian revolution.

There was some luck on Sukarno's side. Much of Indonesia was incredibly fertile. An agricultural expert told me: "Poke a stick into the ground, and in a couple of months you've got a tree." The climate was benevolent. Despite this, there were food shortages. Some people died of hunger. Many more who did not die suffered from malnutrition. But throughout much of Indonesia there was usually something to gnaw upon, and in a tropical country there was little need for heavy clothing or substantial houses.

Sukarno scoffed at his foreign critics. "I consider," he told them, "your psychological warfare the barking of a dog. Tens of times you have claimed that Indonesia under Sukarno would flounder, would collapse, would be destroyed. But we are immune. You have predicted the Indonesian economy would collapse. But it did not."

In a sense, he was right. By every normal economic yardstick, Indonesia was bankrupt and on the point of economic collapse, but somehow it teetered onwards.

Foreign exchange was exhausted. A Russian-built steel mill was abandoned and rusting. In Bali I saw a splendid textile mill idle for want of raw material. A canning factory laid off 300 workers because there was no tin. In the cities, the problem was even more acute than in the countryside. For the office worker there was no handy banana tree, no plot where he could grow a little food for his family. The price of rice soared from week to week, but wages remained unmoved. In real money, senior officials were earning the equivalent of a few dollars a month. A friend of mine in a responsible foreign ministry position earned the equivalent of $4.50 a month. Army generals took second jobs. Honest men looked for extra work; dishonest men became corrupt, stole, or took to petty racketeering.

Sukarno urged his people to vary their diet. "I ask you," he said, "to make a sacrifice. Add maize, sweet potatoes, and the like to your menu of rice. Maize is wholesome food. Peanuts are wholesome. Cassava and its leaves are wholesome. I myself eat maize at least once a week."

For a while Sukarno counted on handouts from a string of countries. Indonesia was important to a number of governments. It was big, the fourth most populous country in the world. It had a commanding position astride east-west sea routes. It had acquired a navy and jet bombers from the Soviet Union. But as Sukarno embarked on a more militant foreign policy, aid from foreign countries became more one-sided. Communist countries could support these adventures, Western nations would not. Sukarno adopted a familiar strategy of tyrants, inventing foreign threats. After launching a confrontation with Malaysia, his mobs sacked and set fire to the British embassy in Jakarta. The kilted military attaché, with British aplomb, played the bagpipes and marched up and down as the flames went heavenwards. British aid to Indonesia was halted. The United States canceled a big, pending loan to Indonesia.

Communism's Role

The communists had made two previous sorties into Indonesia. One was in 1926, when 200 armed men assaulted the telephone and telegraph building in Batavia, as the capital was then called. The revolt was quickly put down by the Dutch, who also purged the party elsewhere in the territory.

In 1948, Communist army officers and Communist Party members launched a rebellion at Madiun, in East Java, which was quickly put down by the Indonesian army. One of the party members who slipped out of the country was a young Sumatran named Dipa Nusantara Aidit. After an absence of two years, he returned to his homeland and began a meteoric rise in the Communist Party of Indonesia (PKI), seizing control of the politburo, and becoming secretary-general of the party at the age of thirty-one. Within a few years, he had made it the third-largest Communist party in the world, ranking only after the parties of the Soviet Union and China. To achieve such growth, Aidit had made a series of interesting compromises, subscribing to Sukarno's *Pantja Sila* platform: belief in God, nationalism, humanism, democracy, and social justice.

When I interviewed Aidit in 1964 at the party's wooden headquarters building in Jakarta, he boasted of his party's success in recruiting good, practicing Muslims: "If a party member wants to go to a mosque or church we let them go." As we talked, workmen hammered away outside and swung girders up and down the multi-story adjacent building that was to be the party's new headquarters. Little did I know that in a year Aidit would be dead, the wooden building in which we talked would be burned to the ground by angry anticommunists, and the big new concrete office block next door would be turned over to the Indonesian maritime ministry for its use.

I asked Aidit whether he was satisfied with his party's then legitimate but limited role in President Sukarno's government. "What party," he countered, "is ever satisfied? We think the strength of our party entitles us to a bigger say in government than we have now."

Clearly he was confident of his party's role, and enjoyed the importance of his position as leader of the largest communist party in the noncommunist world. Our interview was brought to a close by the arrival of a large black Mercedes bearing diplomatic plates. "Now," he said with a smile, "I must receive the Soviet ambassador. Print in your newspaper that I receive the Soviet ambassador." He did not tell me, as I was to discover later, that he was informing the Soviet ambassador that the Indonesian party, because of its pro-Chinese line, would not be attending a conference of world Communist parties in Moscow. As I left, I heard him explaining in English to the Soviet ambassador: "I am being interviewed by the *Christian Science Monitor*."

Despite its skillful leadership and energetic organization, the Indonesian Communist Party could not have reached the importance it did without two other factors. The first of these was the country's increasingly desperate economic crisis. The second was President Sukarno's own political slide toward the left. On the occasion of Indonesia's independence anniversary on August 17, 1964, Sukarno lashed out publicly at the United States. China's foreign minister, Marshal Chen Yi, had just visited Sukarno and the anti-American line was set.

Aidit embraced the new line eagerly. For Sukarno it was a splendid foreign issue to divert attention from the economic chaos at home. For Aidit, it whipped up the ferment on which his Communist Party thrived. Every setback for the United States in Indonesia was a step forward for the communists.

As the relationship between Washington and Jakarta cooled, U.S. aid to Indonesia trickled to a virtual halt. In December the balloon went up. The anti-American campaign exploded in ugly violence at the USIS cultural center in Jakarta. With no warning, a crowd of 300 surrounded the building and started smashing windows. Known members of the Communist youth organization were in the ranks of the rioters. The attackers poured in, overturning bookcases, hurling books out of the windows, and setting them alight on a huge bonfire. They tore down from a wall the seal of the USIS and smashed it to pieces. They ripped apart a picture of President Lyndon Johnson, and destroyed posters for the John F. Kennedy commemorative film, *Years of Lightning, Day of Drums.* I had watched the film only a few nights before at the home of an American diplomat, where Indonesian guests had wept with grief at Kennedy's assassination.

Surging through the wrecked downstairs library, the mob made for the American flag hanging from a second-floor flagstaff. They tore it to shreds and flung the pieces on the flaring bonfire below. Then they hoisted the Indonesian flag in place of the desecrated American one. It was a thoroughly nasty, well-planned affair, designed to inflame American feelings and send Indonesian-American relations plunging. It was a pattern to become all too familiar in the

48

following months. Four days after the USIS center in Jakarta was sacked, a thousand anti-American rioters hacked their way into the USIS library in Surabaya, Indonesia's second largest city and major port, duplicating the Jakarta attack in every way.

Thereafter, the U.S. embassy, its consulates in outlying cities, and USIS libraries around the country, were to become regular targets of leftist and Communist mobs. At the embassy in Jakarta, the doors would be slammed shut with weary monotony, the gates of the courtyard locked. Embassy staff would be mustered on the top floor. The marine guards would break out their tear-gas masks and riot equipment in case the mobs should break through the glass doors. Soon workmen began building a huge grille across the whole front of the building.

In a country where Sukarno ruled all, it seemed clear that if he had not personally ordered the anti-American onslaught, he was at least allowing it to continue. The American ambassador, Howard Jones, pressed his protests and demanded apologies. Despite his once warm relationship with Jones, Sukarno did not deign to reply with even an informal message of regret.

At loggerheads with the Americans, already at war with the British for their backing of a new Malaysian federation, over his head in debt to the Soviets, Sukarno was fast running out of allies. But brighter and brighter on his horizon dawned the red star of Communist China. Increasingly, Sukarno talked of a Peking-Jakarta axis. Into his speeches there crept more and more frequent references to "turning the steering wheel" of his country, and "swinging the helm over."

Though Sukarno spurned the representatives of the West, the Chinese ambassador to Indonesia was a frequent and welcome visitor to the presidential palace. For advice on foreign affairs Sukarno leaned more and more on Communist Party leader Aidit.

When Malaysia was seated on the UN Security Council, Sukarno threw a tantrum and withdrew Indonesia from the UN. Most of the world deplored his action. China applauded.

As the months rolled by there was more and more good news for Communist China out of Sukarno's capital. American rubber and oil companies were placed under government control. With most of its libraries seized or sacked, the USIS decided to close up operations and go home. The Peace Corps left too.

American movies were outlawed. Communist unions cut off water and electricity to American homes. Mail was left undelivered. Along the main streets huge anti-American posters showed Uncle Sam getting a crude comeuppance— usually at the end of a sharpened bamboo stake. The shrinking American community found Indonesian friends less and less eager to talk or visit.

Ambassador Jones was coming to the end of his seven-year assignment. His successor, Marshall Green, arrived to a flurry of posters along the road from the airport advising him to go home. The new ambassador found Jakarta beginning to assume an air of international intrigue, as foreign governments and their agents tried to unravel the mystery of Indonesia's intentions. The Americans watched the Russians. The Russians watched the Chinese. The British, burned out of their embassy by Communist mobs, worked from their ambassador's residence, watching everybody. The West Germans, who had an embassy in Jakarta, watched the East Germans, who had a consulate. The West Germans were building a handsome new embassy building and were in anguish lest Indonesia should recognize East Germany before they could get it finished.

Probably the most frustrated of all were the Soviets. They had given Indonesia massive military and economic assistance. They had built a huge showpiece sports stadium for the Indonesians. Yet Sukarno did not seem to have learned how to play the game—at least the way the Soviets thought it should be played.

This time it was not the Americans thwarting Moscow's ambitions, but the Chinese Communists. The Chinese maintained their embassy—secretive, austere, far removed from everybody else's—down in the Glodok Chinese quarter of Jakarta. The gates were kept locked, there was barbed wire atop the high red walls, and the visitors least welcome were the Soviets.

So the Soviets fretted in their embassy on exclusive diplomatic row. It was a pastel mansion, very bourgeois, with colored fairy lights trimming the façade, and a compound with swimming pool and tennis courts where the diplomats could work off their frustrations and ponder the fickleness of Sukarno, who had gobbled up their aid, then allied himself with Peking (now Beijing). As a Russian correspondent told me glumly over lunch: "Those Chinese are *everywhere*. But we can never find out what they are *doing*."

As we learned later, one of the things the Chinese were doing was negotiating a deal with Omar Dhani, the Communist-leaning chief of the Indonesian air force, who had been sent by Sukarno on a secret mission to Peking. The mission was to arrange the shipment of 100,000 Chinese small arms into Indonesia without informing the army or regular defense ministry officials.

As Sukarno leaned more and more leftwards, he had become increasingly critical of the generals of his army who were largely anti-Communist. In one of his speeches he pointed a not-too-subtle finger at them: "Those who were revolutionary yesterday are possibly counterrevolutionary today," he said. "Even if you were formerly a bald-headed general in 1945 (during Indonesia's fight for independence), if you split the revolutionary national unity today, if you are an enemy of the main pillars of revolution today, then you have become a force of reaction."

Although Sukarno said it was his idea, the Communists pressed for a "fifth force" of peasant militia. The army was under no illusions about it. They believed it would be a Communist force, ending the army's influence, and putting the country within Communism's grasp. The generals' suspicions were not allayed by a series of fiery speeches demanding the crushing of the "capitalist bureaucrats." In the tortuous phraseology of Indonesian politics, everybody knew that meant the army generals blocking the Communists, and apparently the president's, way.

As political tensions rose, the Communist-backing Front Pemuda demanded mass action against "corruptors, capitalist bureaucrats, pilferers, and charlatans," saying they should be "dragged to the gallows" or "shot in public."

To all this political tension was added a further unsettling factor: the uncertainty of the president's health. Sukarno's kidneys had for months featured in the political dispatches of various embassies in Jakarta to their foreign ministries. That he had kidney trouble was not in dispute. Just how serious it was, and thus how much of a political factor, nobody could be sure. To treat his ailment Sukarno had imported a team of specialists in acupuncture from China. It was widely believed that the Chinese doctors reported to PKI leader Aidit on the state of the president's health. If they reported that Sukarno's illness was serious, or that he could die soon, this was information of tremendous significance that might have impelled the Indonesian Communist Party to emergency action.

It is hardly surprising that this unsettled atmosphere spawned whispers of coups and plots. The army distrusted the Communists. The Communists distrusted the army. The president was leaning ever leftwards, delivering barely disguised criticism of his generals, and awaiting the arrival of 100,000 small arms from China that the generals were not to know about. The Communists began to privately spread the word that a "Council of Generals" was plotting against the president. The army leadership got whispers that the Communists were planning a coup against it.

September 30, 1965

For a night destined to change the course of history, it began innocently enough. As the day's heat ebbed, a misty blue twilight settled over Jakarta in brief, mellow transition before the onrush of tropical darkness. The moon that rose with nightfall was peaceful, pale, and full. As the day's gasoline fumes faded, the liberated evening air took on a gentle fragrance peculiar to Indonesia, an exotic blend of jasmine, frangipani, and the smoke from locally made cigarettes spiced with cloves.

But it was all tension that evening at Halim air force base, on the southern outskirts of Jakarta. Around 10 p.m., a column of troops rolled in from Jakarta. There was the clink of metal and weapons, the subdued bark of urgent orders, the confused expletives as officers sought their rendezvous points in the dark on an air force base strange to most of them.

A little after this, a tan military jeep with a canvas roof sped down the road from Jakarta carrying the two main figures in the coup that was about to take place. One was Lieutenant Colonel Untung bin Syamsuri, a battalion commander of the presidential palace guard, the Tjakrabirawa. He had only one serious blot on his record. He had fought briefly with the Communists when they staged an abortive revolt in the East Javanese town of Madiun back in 1948.

The other was Brigadier-General Mustafa Sjarif Supardjo, a former regimental commander of the army's Siliwangi division, stationed in West Java. He had been in trouble with his commanders for pro-Communist sympathies and actions. He had been sent off to the jungles of Kalimantan, far from the capital, to take part in operations against British and Malaysian troops along the border between Malaysian and Indonesian territory. He had left his post, unknown to his superiors, and flown to Jakarta, ostensibly to come home because his child was ill. He had received a cable from his wife to this effect, but at his trial later it was revealed this was a code agreed upon earlier between Supardjo and Communist participants in the about-to-take-place coup. The real reason for his return was that he was to play a commanding role in the plot. The plan was to murder the army's high command and take over the government.

The air force base had been a hotbed of Communist activity for some time. When the communists sought to secretly train a force of their own shock troops, drawn from their youth organization, the Pemuda Rakjat, they did so on a remote part of the base. Sympathetic air force officers gave them weapons and training. Their own instructors gave them political indoctrination.

Several thousand of these Communist shock troops, along with Untung's battalion of palace guards and two

Communist-infiltrated army battalions from Central and East Java (each about 1,000 men strong), in town for an armed forces day parade, were the units to carry out the plan.

By 4 a.m. the seven squads assigned to seize the targeted generals were in position outside their homes in Jakarta. Only two of the houses had military guards to be overpowered. At each residence, the invading soldiers began their murderous assignment. The most senior general, Nasution, got away from the troops who broke into his house. But in throwing himself over a wall he broke his ankle. His five-year-old daughter was shot and later died. Of the other six generals targeted, three were killed when they resisted. Three were taken alive, along with a young military aide from General Nasution's house. The bodies and captured officers were driven to Halim air force base and the remote Communist training area. There they were savagely mutilated, the survivors killed, the bodies thrown down a well.

In the first stages of the coup attempt, the plotters had made two major blunders. They had bungled the capture of General Nasution, and they had not put General Suharto on the priority list of generals to be neutralized first. Suharto was commander of KOSTRAD, the army's strategic reserve. He had spent the night with his son fishing where a river surged down to the sea. When he and his son returned home early the next morning he found his household in confusion. Aides had a jumbled account of what happened to the other generals, and of a Communist coup, and even uncertainty as to whether Sukarno himself had been killed.

The coup leaders announced on radio that they had thwarted a plot by army generals to seize power, would continue to purge other army elements, and were setting up a Revolutionary Council headed by Untung and Supardjo.

Suharto took control of the army and set about determining which units were loyal and which were not. He located General Nasution and brought him to safety at KOSTRAD headquarters. Sukarno, meanwhile, had taken up sanctuary at Halim air force base, along with Aidit.

Within 24 hours, Suharto had broken the back of the coup, stabilized the situation, and neutralized the rebel forces in Jakarta. He ordered an attack on Halim air base, which was taken with only modest resistance. The rebels were in retreat. Air force chief Dhani had sent Aidit on an air force plane to Jogjakarta in Central Java. Sukarno had left by car for a destination then unknown.

The capital remained tense. Strongpoints and communications centers were encircled by barbed wire barricades. At key crossroads, tough Indonesian soldiers sat atop tanks and armored cars. From Merdeka Square, the central square on one side of which stood the presidential palace, the barrels of antiaircraft guns ranged upward in pointed skepticism of the air force's loyalty.

Telephone and cable traffic to the outside world was cut off. Within the city, local telephones were "presently disconnected." To talk to anybody, you had to visit them. You could do this only during the hours of daylight, for the army had imposed a curfew from 6 at night till 6 in the morning. After darkness the streets were left to jeeps and trucks, carrying loyalist troops on official business.

There now occurred one of the most inexplicable developments in the whole affair. The day after General Suharto had clearly smashed the "September 30th Movement,"as it was called, the Communist Party newspaper, *Hurian Rakjat*, went on the capital's streets with an editorial supporting the movement. It was an act of incredible political stupidity which was to set the seal on the party's fate.

The editorial claimed the September 30th Movement was in fact launched to foil a coup by the army's generals. It said "the sympathy and support of the people is surely on the side of the September 30th Movement." To quell any doubts about the Communist Party's position, there was a crude, front-page cartoon showing a mighty fist, labeled "September 30th Movement," smashing into the face of an Indonesian general. The general's pockets were stuffed with money bills, he had dollar signs for epaulettes, his cap was stamped with the initials "CIA." Propping him up was a particularly unpleasant-looking Uncle Sam. A second picture showed a pair of generals, with dollars and CIA labels flying, being tossed on to a row of bayonets and sharpened stakes.

The editorial was probably written, and the paper set and printed, late the previous afternoon when the Communists thought the coup attempt was moving successfully. Why the Communists did not prevent its distribution the following morning remains a mystery. But this public Communist Party endorsement of the coup, and the murder of its generals, enraged the surviving generals and provided the documentary evidence for the party's coming obliteration.

The Purge

Although the whereabouts of generals Nasution and Suharto were not made public, they were living and sleeping in the days after the abortive coup at the guarded KOSTRAD headquarters. Sukarno's whereabouts were unknown but the radio broadcast a message from him saying he was "safe and well" and continued to "hold the top leadership of the state and government." He said Suharto was "to carry out the restoration of security" and that charges against the air force of involvement in the September 30th Movement were not true.

But Suharto's men were at the Halim air force base looking for the bodies of the murdered generals. They found the well and the bodies. Suharto was shaken with rage and emotion but was under orders from Sukarno not to let the army take bloody vengeance upon the air force. "You can imagine the fury of a soldier," he said later. But his aim was "to keep a tight rein on undisciplined acts by our own boys."

The murdered generals were given a massive funeral, attended by thousands of mourners. General Nasution appeared, under heavy guard, hobbling on sticks. The American and British ambassadors were prominent. Pointedly absent were diplomatic representatives of Communist China. So was Sukarno. General Suharto, dressed in battle fatigues, stamped around, his face heavy with anger. He was not a man on this day to be interfered with. To the army's elite RPKAD paracommandos were given the honor of carrying the coffins of the generals and Nasution's young aide to their final resting places.

By morning of the next day, the mystery of Sukarno's whereabouts was solved. He was at the weekend palace of Bogor, some 40 miles from the capital, and he had called a meeting of his cabinet. Although there was a ban on press interviews, I found myself seated 3 feet across from him, the man who could unravel many mysteries of the past few days. He was joking and laughing with some of his ministers. Communist Party members of his cabinet were present.

"What words do you have for the press?" I asked him.

"Just a smile," he replied.

"We note the smile, but would prefer some words," I said. He laughed, and some members of his cabinet joined in. I tried a couple more questions. He clucked and shook his head, saying: "You are angling me (*sic*). These correspondents have very many tricks, many difficult questions." He was not to be drawn out and aides ushered us out.

After the cabinet meeting concluded, Foreign Minister Subandrio informed reporters that the president had told the cabinet he did not condone the murders or the establishment of the Revolutionary Council. But if we were to believe the words dropping from Subandrio's lips, Sukarno seemed to be absolving the Communist Party from all blame.

The army was astonished and enraged at Sukarno's mild reaction to events. Sukarno had not been present at the funeral of his generals. Now he was trying to shelter the Communists.

From Nasution there was no lead. He was plunged into his own personal trauma of grief. Although he was defense minister he had stayed away from the cabinet meeting at Bogor. His daughter had died from her wounds on that very day.

Suharto had heeded the president's injunction to maintain peace and had prevented his men from assaulting the air force. But now his patience was at an end. He and the generals around him had abundant evidence of Communist involvement in the September 30th Movement. With or without Sukarno's authorization, they were now determined to grind the Communist Party into oblivion. With cold, relentless fury they set about the task.

At the funeral of Nasution's 5-year-old daughter, Admiral Eddy Martadinata, head of the navy, passed the word to anti-Communist student leaders. As he brushed by them, from the corner of his mouth he spat out a single word, "*Sikat.*" They had no difficulty in grasping his meaning. The word means "sweep." The message was that they could go out and clean up the Communists without any hindrance from the military. With relish they called out their followers, stuck their knives and pistols in their waistbands, swung their clubs over their shoulders, and set about their assignment. The morning after the funeral, demonstrators marched on Communist Party headquarters. As they went, they tore down pro-Communist signs and scribbled on walls and fences: "Crush the PKI" and "Kill Aidit." At the building where less than a year ago I had chatted with Aidit, they smashed the interior to pieces, then put the building to the torch. Three fire trucks were in attendance, but they waited till only the ashes were left before they went into action.

Thousands of demonstrators were now in the streets. As army trucks passed they cheered, stopped them, and shook hands with the soldiers. More anti-Communist slogans were pasted on the windshields of cars. As the trucks and cars rattled past the American embassy, there were even shouts of "Long live America."

The wrath of the crowds was not only directed at the Communist Party. China's diplomats had been ostentatious by their absence from the funeral of the army's heroes. Now they refused to obey the army's order to fly all flags at half-mast in a period of mourning. As I checked, the flag of Communist China flew defiantly from the top of the embassy flagpole. Soon the demonstrators were parading outside all Chinese diplomatic offices and residences. Two thousand demonstrators stormed the Chinese consulate in Medan, in northern Sumatra. The anger spilled over against resident Chinese businessmen and traders who, like many Chinese communities throughout Southeast Asia, by dint of their industry and capital had acquired a dominant role in the country's economic life.

As the anti-Chinese campaign picked up steam, China cut off its military aid to Indonesia and halted trade. Their technicians were withdrawn and called back to China. But if Indonesia's relations with China were now in the deep freeze, the army was bent on ruthlessly dismantling the entire Communist Party organization at home. Gruesome photographs of the murdered generals' bodies were quietly circulated throughout military ranks. Now a sinister new word—*Gestapu*—was coined from the initials of the name *September 30th Movement, Gerakan September Tiga Puluh*.

Whatever Sukarno thought, the army was writing its own orders. Operating under a "state of war," it announced a "military ban" on the Communist Party in Jakarta. Thousands of Communists and suspects were scooped up. Fifty-seven Communist members of parliament were "suspended." Aidit's house in Jakarta was demolished completely, brick by brick and tile by tile. Commanders in other parts of the country followed suit. Communist mayors in a string of cities were dismissed or imprisoned.

While Jakarta was the focal point of the *Gestapu* operation, the plotters had also struck in various parts of the country. For the most part, disloyal troops or units were easily put down. But in the central region of Indonesia's major island of Java, the *Gestapu* forces made a formidable stand. This was the stronghold of the Communist Party. It had too many people on too little land and had been easy prey for the Communists with their heady promises of land reform. It was to this region that Aidit fled after the collapse of *Gestapu* in Jakarta. The Communists had also infiltrated the Diponegoro division of the army, stationed in central Java.

After Suharto had consolidated his hold on the capital, General Sarwo Edhy, the commander of the elite RPKAD paracommandos, was dispatched with his men to central Java. His mission was to put down any lingering disloyal military units and then, by whatever means necessary, terminate the Communist Party there. As he told me later, the area was too big and too crowded for him to distribute his forces effectively. "We decided to encourage the anticommunist civilians to help with the job. We gathered together the youth, the nationalist groups, the religious organizations. We gave them two or three days training, then sent them out to kill the communists."

Thus began Indonesia's postcoup bloodbath.

Untung, who had commanded the units that seized the army's top generals, was arrested near his hometown of Tegal, in central Java, and later stood trial. Aidit was captured hiding in a small house near Solo, also in central Java, by Sarwo Edhy's paracommandos. He was killed, but Sarwo Edhy would not reveal how, nor where his body might be buried. The army wanted no legend built around Aidit, nor shrine to mark his grave.

In the mass killings that took place, old grudges were settled, and false information was given about people who may or may not have been active Communist Party members.

So many people were killed that there was a problem disposing of the bodies. Many were flung into rivers and washed out to sea. In the port city of Surabaya, the British consul found several bodies on the riverbank next to his garden.

The paracommandos swept through Java throughout October and November of 1965 and on to Bali in December, where the harsh ideology of Communism had made serious inroads into an island of deep Hindu belief, artistic bent, and ancient traditions. The Communist Party recruited members in Bali who sometimes were Communists of a most nominal kind.

But later Sarwo Edhy told me that while "in Java we had to egg the people on to kill Communists, in Bali we had to restrain them, make sure they didn't go too far."

In the last three months of 1965, it is clear that Indonesia was swept by a massacre of staggering proportions. Estimates of how many people were killed vary, some as high as a million, some as low as 60,000, with "popular" estimates polarizing around 400,000. My own estimate was around 200,000. However an official nine-man investigating commission reported to President Sukarno that 78,000 people had lost their lives. When Sukarno publicly announced the figures from their report, he squinted through his spectacles, got the first two figures transposed, and declared that the toll was 87,000. Reporters present sent that figure around the world.

When I talked with one of the commission members later, I asked whether he was satisfied with the accuracy of the figure 78,000 they had offered. "Of course not," he told me. "It was probably about ten times that figure—780,000." So why did they report 78,000? With that cheerful Indonesian capacity for bemusing and confounding the Westerner's mind, he explained: "Sukarno was still in charge. We gave him the figures we thought he wanted to hear."

The Fall of Sukarno

As 1965 drifted into 1966, Sukarno and the army presided over Indonesia in a sort of uneasy coalition rule.

The army had assumed sweeping emergency powers. To Sukarno it was an unwelcome poacher upon his authority. Yet with the Communist Party virtually obliterated, he had no other instrument at hand with which to cut back the army to size.

For its part, the army leadership was increasingly disillusioned with Sukarno. Nasution and Suharto were suspicious of his role in the coup attempt and disgusted that he had dragged his feet in the condemnation and punishment of Communists afterwards.

But if disillusionment had set in, the army was reluctant to confront Sukarno directly. Sukarno was revered as the father of the nation. About him there was a legendary aura. Could the army challenge his prestige and influence and get away with it? He had solid support in large areas of central and east Java. Though the soldiers were now considered the heroes of the anti-Communist cause, their massacre of Communists had also made them many enemies.

The ranks of government were strewn with senior officials who had prospered on Sukarno's patronage and would be alarmed to see him go. Within the army even, many generals owed their positions to Sukarno. Some of them were flatly opposed to any talk of ousting him.

Now into this tense political situation was injected a new political factor—the teenage students of Jakarta who were fed up with the economic chaos they were falling heir to and for whom the magic of Sukarno had worn transparently thin. Born after the revolution of 1945, they had no personal experience of Sukarno's role in it. After 20 years of Indonesian independence, the promised land seemed nowhere in sight.

They poured into the streets, not demonstrating openly against Sukarno but against rising prices and government inefficiency. As the protest movement gained momentum, Sukarno became angrier. But anti-Sukarno slogans began appearing on walls. One weekend the students rumbled off in a convoy to Bogor, demonstrating so noisily at the presidential palace that presidential guards fired shots in the air.

Sukarno told students they should form a "Sukarno Front" to check attempts to overthrow him and prevent the Indonesian revolution being moved to the right. Then he moved sensationally onto the offensive. He shuffled his cabinet, eliminating General Nasution as defense minister and reinstating Omar Dhani, the former air force chief whose role in the *Gestapu* affair had enraged the army, along with Communist Party members.

The intent was to move Indonesia sharply to the left again. But Sukarno had miscalculated the tenacity of the student movement. Now was to be unleashed a campaign of remarkable student intensity, bolstered by the army, that would compel Sukarno to step down.

Demonstrations against the *Gestapu* cabinet, as it was called, became so huge and raucous that the army had again to impose a curfew. By day the protesters brought the work of the capital to a standstill. When you talked to student leaders they wanted three things: the *Gestapu* cabinet out, the Communist Party banned, and prices lowered.

The day before installation of the new cabinet, 50,000 students tried to storm Sukarno's palace in the heart of Jakarta. In the melee some students were injured. Next day, as the new cabinet was due to be installed, the students stopped every car and every truck at every intersection in the city. They slewed the vehicles across the roads and let the air out of their tires. Hundreds of vehicles blocked the streets for hours. It was a well-conceived plan, that brought Jakarta to a standstill, intended to prevent the new cabinet ministers reaching the palace. No cars could fetch the stranded ministers, and they would have to be brought in by helicopters.

Finally the cabinet ministers were flown in. Outside, the students were pushing the presidential guard. Suddenly there was the crackle of automatic gunfire. One of the victims was a medical student shot dead. In that instant the student campaign was transformed. Now the students had their political martyr.

In the days and weeks ahead, Jakarta was the scene of civil war as the students, both university and high school, demonstrated. Fifty thousand turned out for the funeral of the slain student. An enraged Sukarno ordered the University of Indonesia closed. Although theoretically closed, thousands arrived for the inauguration of a new student "regiment." Rival forces from the leftist Bung Karno University were now in the streets, along with gangs unleashed by the new security affairs minister. The streets were now very dangerous as it was not always easy to distinguish which group of demonstrators was which. While one anti-Sukarno group attacked and occupied the foreign ministry, about 200 leftists swarmed into the grounds of the American embassy, smashing windows and firebombing embassy cars. The day after the attack on the American embassy, anti-Communist demonstrators stormed the New China News Agency offices and later the Chinese consular offices.

A rattled Sukarno summoned his new cabinet to his palace. The meeting was disrupted when the presidential guard commander hurried into the room and handed the president a handwritten note. It said that unidentified troops had the palace surrounded and were advancing. Sukarno reacted quickly, leaving his cabinet behind, and making for his helicopter on the palace lawn, always ready for flight. Within minutes he was whirling away. The unidentified troops were in fact Sarwo Edhy's paracommandos, stripped of their insignia. Months later, Sarwo Edhy told me drily: "We didn't advertise the fact. We weren't wearing our red berets."

The denouement was clearly at hand. Halim air base had already been "neutralized" in the event Sukarno sought to go there. Instead he flew to the weekend palace at Bogor. There his palace guard ensured his safety. But Suharto had placed a discreet outer cordon of troops loyal to him around the palace area.

Suharto sent three trusted generals to Bogor to meet with the president. The official line was that the generals "clarified the political and security situation in the country."

In fact they carried a document for Sukarno to sign authorizing General Suharto "to take all steps considered necessary to ensure security, calm and stability of the government." There was also a line instructing Suharto to "guarantee the personal safety" of the president.

The transfer of sweeping authority from Sukarno to Suharto transformed the political atmosphere in Jakarta and forestalled acts of arson, murder, and political assassination planned for the next day. In the early hours of that day, a student contact came hammering on my hotel room door. "We've won, we've won," he cried excitedly. "The president's given in, surrendered, it's all over." Well, not quite.

Now began some months-long maneuvering as Suharto began a campaign to shed the country of Sukarnoism while retaining Sukarno as a figurehead. The Communist Party was banned, the cabinet was purged of Communists and leftists, plans were made to end the war over Malaysia and to return to the UN. The Tjakrabirawa palace guard was disbanded, and Sukarno's helicopters were no longer available, except for trips approved by Suharto. Sukarno was not allowed to slip away to central Java, where he might stir up trouble. Telephone calls from the palace were controlled, and his visitors regulated.

Suharto was insistent on constitutionality and dignity in handling of the president. Privately he told friends he wanted no Latin American–style power takeover in Indonesia. Suharto wanted the People's Consultative Congress, which had been sidelined during Sukarno's rule, revived as the supreme constitutional authority, to which the president would be subservient. Besides, he argued, Sukarno's provocative dismissal could spark violence among his still considerable supporters, perhaps even civil war.

The Congress was revived. General Nasution, now speaking out increasingly critically of the old Sukarno order, was elected its chairman. But Sukarno was unwilling to become a sort of grand old man of the Indonesian revolution. He fought back, clawed at the new leadership, contradicting its reassuring statements to the outside world. "I am a Marxist," he declared. "Marxism is in my chest," even though the Congress had banned Marxism. As the army counseled patience, the students were out in mass in the streets again, demanding Sukarno's ouster. Finally the Congress announced that Sukarno had "failed to meet his constitutional responsibilities," and he was stripped of his powers. Suharto was appointed acting president.

Suharto Takes Hold

The following year, General Suharto was formally installed president of Indonesia, to remain such for the next three decades. For those who hoped his presidency would usher in an era of democracy, he proved a major disappointment. With the attempted coup still fresh in his mind, he maintained the army as a bulwark against any resurgence of Communism or emergence of any new challenge to the government. The army's dominance of politics was ensured by its control of a new party, Golkar, speaking largely with the voice of the military and positioned to dominate other minority parties permitted to exist. The army had a key role in all branches of governmental bureaucracy throughout the far-flung regions of the Indonesian archipelago.

Suharto's main achievement in office was to galvanize the economy that President Sukarno had allowed to verge upon collapse. For almost Suharto's entire presidency, the economy grew by an average of 7 percent a year. Although this was a boon to some of the country's poor, key beneficiaries were Suharto family members and cronies who occupied lucrative roles in new business monopolies. This was not penny-ante corruption, but corruption on a massive scale, siphoning off billions of dollars. With mounting resentment against corruption in high places and an authoritarian regime in power, economic disaster rolled in upon Indonesia with the 1997 Asian financial crisis. Soaring inflation and unemployment triggered massive demonstrations and riots in various parts of the nation. Suharto was forced to resign and was briefly succeeded by his vice president, B.J. Habibie, who eased restrictions on the media and political parties.

Now Indonesians were finally to embark on the path of free elections, long denied them. In a period of some six years they were to undergo a transformation from near-dictatorship to vigorous democracy. For three of those years their president was Megawati Sukarnoputri, Sukarno's daughter. She presided over a period of some political stability but did not prove dynamic in addressing the country's problems.

In her cabinet, serving as coordinating minister for political and security affairs, was Susilo Bambang Yudhoyono, a well-regarded former army general. In 2004, in a complex new electoral process, capped by the nation's first direct presidential election, he ran against her and won a handsome victory. Running on an anticorruption platform, he won reelection to the presidency again in 2009 with a resounding vote of confidence.

Since then, Indonesia has made progress on several major challenges.

Yudhoyono has not yet achieved his goal of ridding the nation of the "legal mafia," a reference to pervasive corruption in the judiciary and law enforcement. A political scandal in 2009 revealed sabotage of the highly respected anticorruption agency, the Corruption Eradication Commission, by top officials in the police and attorney general's office. But Yudhoyono's war on corruption remains a top priority.

In a far-flung archipelago of diverse factions, the threat of remote provinces breaking away from the Javanese-dominated center was real. But an ambitious decentralization has lessened that prospect. Yudhoyono is proud of a peace agreement with Aceh, an oil-rich province in northern Sumatra. Rebels there ceased their fight for independence in return for a role in the politics and government of the territory. Papua, at the eastern end of the culturally and ethnically diverse Indonesian archipelago, was granted similar autonomy in the program of decentralization from the central government.

Despite his military background, SBY, as he is generally known in Indonesia, has made it clear that the army should curb its long role in civilian affairs. But though the army may be more in the background today than in previous years, it is retained as a vigorous entity, ready to be deployed against any force threatening the nation's stability, whether it be the Communism or Marxism of the past or the Islamic terrorism of the present.

After independence, a series of authoritarian regimes and a serious Communist-attempted takeover did serious damage to the legitimacy of state government in Indonesia, providing a fertile field for radical Islam. But it has emerged as one of the stablest, if not the stablest, nations in Southeast Asia. Despite some lingering aberrations like the banning of books dealing too clinically with the problems of the past, its people enjoy free elections, free speech, and a free press.

PART
III

Indonesia:
An Example for Islam?

*"If you want to know whether Islam, democracy, modernity,
and women's rights can co-exist, go to Indonesia."*

HILLARY CLINTON

IN SOME RESPECTS Indonesia might seem an ideal target
for the expansion of Al-Qaeda-backed or directed terrorism. Indonesia is the largest Muslim country in the
world, with porous borders and large regions of poverty.
Indeed, the hand of Jemaah Islamiyah, a militant Islamic
group active in several Southeast Asian countries that seeks
to establish a pan-Islamic state across the region, and a
more extreme splinter group, is evident in several terrorist
attacks that have taken place in Indonesia. These include
the bombing of a night club on Bali which killed more than
200 people, a suicide car bombing outside the Australian

embassy, and an assault on J.W. Marriott and Ritz-Carlton hotels in Jakarta.

But deplorable though these actions were, they are not of the scale or frequency of terrorist attacks that have taken place in lands elsewhere. The reasons for this are several.

Indonesia's brand of Islam is more moderate than that practiced in other Muslim states where Islamic extremists have been able to breed and recruit. Though some militant groups have attempted to impose the concept of *sharia* law, as practiced in other Muslim nations, they have gained little traction in Indonesia. There is no official mosque or spiritual leader. Yudhoyono's government presides over a mix of predominantly secular and Islamic minority groups that are fully protected. Particularly meaningful is the protection of a significant Chinese minority active, as in other Southeast Asian countries, in trade and commerce. During the purge following the *Gestapu* coup attempt, the Chinese were often singled out as targets. The tolerance and moderation of Indonesia's Muslim faith today has proved fallow ground for Islamist jihad.

After years of violence and autocratic rule, Indonesia revels in its newfound democracy. Voting is free and fair; President Yudhoyono, having been first elected in 2004, was reelected to another term in 2009. Hard-line Islamic parties were able to campaign and did so, but none provided any serious competition. As Joshua Kurlantzick, a Southeast Asia Fellow at the Council on Foreign Relations, wrote: "Though Indonesian leaders themselves are hesitant to lecture other countries, their model could offer lessons for nations from Pakistan to Morocco. [Indonesia] has managed to create a stable political system using its military to guarantee secular rule, as does Turkey. The militant Islamic groups that might have emerged to threaten the country's future have been crushed and co-opted. Indonesia has adopted modern techniques that appear to be working. In its success, Indonesia also offers the United States ways to help build stable societies in the Arab-Muslim world. It is a model for cooperation and moderation."[1]

Then there are the lessons of history. Although the Indonesian students of the Sukarno era, and the bloody purge that followed it, are today ageing and silver haired, the horror of those events is as fresh as yesterday, a searing memory on the nation's psyche. There is a "never again" mechanism that kicks in and rejects any concept of more mass violence.

Tackling the problems of backwardness and poverty, so often the breeding ground for terrorism in the Arab world, the Indonesian government has embarked on a massive antipoverty campaign, funneling cash and benefits to the poor. One of the reasons enabling the now-discredited Communist Party in Indonesia to recruit so heavily in the 1960s was its distribution of seed and rice to peasant farmers at huge discounts from prices demanded by banks and lenders.

The government has also tamped down secessionist leanings in outer regions of the Indonesian archipelago by a policy of decentralization, giving them more local autonomy and control over local finances.

Another tool in the government's panoply for stability is a large standing army. While the army's political influence has been toned down, it remains a force at the government's hand should need arise to quell any unwelcome threat to Indonesia's peaceful progress from without or within. The army has not been assigned to hunt Islamic terrorists, the police force having proved extremely successful in this effort.

From the outset of his tenure, President Yudhoyono made the defeat of terrorism an important priority of his administration. In public speeches he made clear to his people that the terrorists were a threat to Indonesians, as well as to Westerners, and that they must be liquidated and Indonesian youth protected from recruitment. He urged the "whole of the Indonesian people" to rise up against terrorists and promoted an organization, "Terror Free Tomorrow," an overwhelming majority of which declared that terrorism was unjustified under any circumstances. The president of one of Indonesia's largest Muslim organizations, Kiai Haj Hasyim Muzadi, declared: "Terrorism has nothing to do with Islam."

While some were killed in firefights, the authorities have captured more than 300 terrorists, trying them in the courts, which sentenced them to jail or execution. But the government has also launched a remarkable "deradicalisation" program, using former militants to "turn" convicted terrorists in prison, using religion and "soft persuasion" to win them over. Some of the redeemed militants have appeared on television, chronicling, and apologizing for, their violent pasts. Some have cooperated with the police to help find would-be terrorists still at large.

The police, especially an "88" counterterrorism unit, have developed skills in intelligence and tracking that have hobbled nascent terrorist plans. In 2009 the 88 unit trapped and killed Noordin Mohammed Top, one of the most wanted terrorist leaders in Indonesia, if not Southeast Asia. Noordin had broken away from Jemaah Islamiyah to form a splinter group loyal to Al Qaeda, marginalizing him and making him even more repugnant to Indonesians as a violent extremist of the radical fringe. He had evaded capture on a number of occasions. While the mainstream Jemaah Islamiyah had backed away from supporting violence, Top had not. Sidney Jones, an expert on Indonesian terrorism with the International Crisis Group, said Top was the only leading militant leader in Indonesia still campaigning for implementation of Osama bin Laden's 1998 fatwa on killing Westerners.[2] The Malaysian-born Top had built up something of a cult among some younger militants, contemptuous of many senior members of Jemaah Islamiyah, dismissing them as NATO—"No Action, Talk Only." Top's death was seen as a major blow for extremist organizations in Indonesia.

One more positive factor in their campaign is that the Indonesians have tackled their terrorism problem without a large American footprint in place. There has been quiet American help in some areas of training with the 88 unit, but there has been no requirement, or wish for, American troops on the ground.

The American role in Indonesia's affairs has not been trumpeted. This serves both countries well. Some conspiracy theorists have sought to depict the hand of the CIA in Indonesia, as far back as the days of *Gestapu*. As an eye-witness to those events, I am confident that the United States had no such role. Indonesians themselves purged their country of Communism. Indonesian nationalism was, and is, resilient and durable. Even if it had been eager to intervene in that era, the United States was unable. Then, as since, U.S. diplomacy toward Indonesia has proved one of the most successful chapters in the contemporary history of American foreign policy in Asia.

When then secretary of state Madeleine Albright visited Indonesia in 1999, she praised Indonesia as a cofounder of the nonaligned movement and a driving force behind the Association of Southeast Asian Nations. She lauded Indonesia as a model of tolerance, of "unity in diversity," as proclaimed in the nation's national motto, "Bhinneka Tunggal Ika."

When Hillary Clinton, secretary of state in the Obama administration, visited Indonesia in 2009, she praised Indonesia's "key role in commitment to 'smart power' in international diplomacy." She pledged her administration's intention to "listen, and support the country that has demonstrated so clearly that Islam, democracy, and modernity can not only coexist but thrive together."

Indonesians have met their challenges by themselves. The United States has understood, offering cooperation and assistance when welcome and appropriate.

President Yudhoyono has had six different educational experiences in the U.S., five of them military and one civilian.

But like Indonesian presidents before him, he has kept his relationship with the United States discreet. Ever since Suharto dragged his country back from a leftist embrace under Sukarno, Indonesian leaders have wanted to preserve a posture of public nonalignment, eschewing any suggestion that they have become puppets of the United States. It is a posture which successive U.S. administrations have wisely respected.

When Indonesia was hit by a giant tsunami crashing across its shores, the United States sent the aircraft carrier *Abraham Lincoln* to help in relief efforts. Fifteen thousand U.S. servicemen took part in an airlift by helicopters from ship to shore, delivering tons of food, water, and other aid to the victims. The U.S. effort was appreciated by the Indonesian government and citizens. Subsequent polls in Indonesia showed a sharp increase in the popularity of America. But at a point in the operation, the Indonesian government politely indicated it was time for American troops to leave Indonesian soil. Without question, the American servicemen were withdrawn. Mission accomplished. Diplomacy positive.

This is the kind of humanitarian American involvement which affords Al Qaeda and its offshoots little opportunity for anti-American propaganda or incitement.

I believe that Indonesia, the largest Muslim, but non-Arab, country in the world, and other non-Arab countries with substantial Muslim populations could play a much more significant role in engaging with Muslim nations that are Arab.

Lee Kuan Yew, former prime minister of neighboring Singapore and considered one of Asia's wise elder statesmen, cites Indonesia as an essential participant in the war against terrorism: "When moderate Muslim governments such as those in Indonesia, Malaysia, the Persian Gulf states, Egypt and Jordan, feel comfortable associating themselves openly with a multilateral coalition against Islamic terrorism, the tide of battle will turn against the extremists."[3]

Hassan Wirajuda, Indonesia's foreign minister from 2001 to 2009, signaled his nation's desire to take a larger role in solving problems of the Islamic world. Countries in the Middle East, he argued, have been so deeply involved in their problems for so long that they can get too focused on specific aspects. The holder of graduate degrees in law and diplomacy from Harvard, the Fletcher School, and Oxford, Wirajuda said: "We who follow events in the Middle East from a distance can see a larger, clearer picture. Hence we are able to produce fresh ideas that might be helpful in the quest for a solution."[4]

With its approach to internal political problems, Indonesia typically adopts the practice of *mushiwara*, the art of bringing everybody together to make decisions by consensus, rather than determining winners and losers. Wirajuda believed that Indonesia could usefully use this technique, for example, to attempt reconciliation between the Palestinian factions of Hamas and Fatah.

President Yudhoyono, while carefully avoiding any move that could mark him a tool of the United States, believes Indonesia's melding of democracy, Islam, and modernity befits his nation for a constructive role in reducing terrorism, "a crime that is neither a holy war nor a struggle for justice."

He believes several things have to happen.

First, he believes world leaders must strengthen the various dialogues already taking place, such as the UN Dialogue Among Civilizations, the Saudi initiative of an Interfaith Conference, and the Global Inter-Media Dialogue (launched by Indonesia after the crisis following cartoon depictions of the Prophet Muhammad).

Second, these efforts must reach deeper to the grassroots. "Even in the most modern societies, ignorance about other religions is commonplace. In some Western countries, Islam is the fastest-growing religion—and this is accompanied by rising Islamophobia. A recent Gallup poll indicated that the proportion of Muslims who understand and appreciate the West is much higher than the number of Westerners who appreciate Islam . . . this is a two-way street. Leaders in the Muslim world must reach out to the West, just as much as they expect the West to understand Islam."

Third, the forces of moderation must be bolstered worldwide. "Tolerance and moderation should be taught to children in schools from a very early age. In Indonesia, Muslim students in school exams are asked questions about the Christian celebration of Christmas, and the Hindu tradition of Nyepi (a day of silence in Bali)."

Fourth, "we will also need to ensure that the world's civilizations can all benefit from globalization. Humanity has never seen a time when all civilizations prosper together. The remedy is education, which will put marginalized socie-

ties on an equal footing with the West in deriving the benefits of civilization."[5]

In lauding Hillary Clinton's decision to visit Indonesia
on her first visit to Asia as secretary of state, the *Atlantic*'s
Robert D. Kaplan wrote: "Indonesia is crucial for many
more reasons than the fact that President Obama went to
school there for a few years as a child. It is the largest Muslim country in the world and the fourth most populous. It
commands the narrow Strait of Malacca, which is the
world's energy highway, where supertankers transport Middle Eastern oil to the burgeoning middle class fleshpots of
the Pacific rim. . . . Indonesia seems to be on its way to
becoming an authentically stable Muslim democracy."

Kaplan argues that if the second Bush presidency was all
about the spread of freedom and democracy, Indonesia per-
fectly followed the former president's example: "It captured, prosecuted and executed the perpetrators of the Bali
terrorist attack of 2002, and then went on to temper the
rages of radicalism through electoral politics. More than
any other country, Indonesia exemplifies Bush's Wilsonian
vision. In Indonesia, Islam is a religion and not a way of
life. It is only one aspect of a heterodox society that still has
Hindu and Buddhist underpinnings from earlier phases of
its history. Radicalized societies like Saudi Arabia and Pakistan represent Islam's past. Indonesia, where Islam must
compete in the battle of ideas with secular and nationalist
ideologies, represents its best case scenario for the future."[6]

Indonesia's history has often been one of adversity: colonization by the Dutch, World War II occupation by the Jap-

anese, Sukarno's flirtation with Communism, the horrors of *Gestapu* and the bloodbath that followed, Suharto's regime of autocratic corruption and a life of poverty and hardship for many, and Islamist terrorism that thankfully has been contained.

Now Indonesians are enjoying a period of relative peace and harmony. As Secretary of State Clinton puts it: "If you want to know whether Islam, democracy, modernity and women's rights can co-exist, go to Indonesia."[7] The nation is emerging as a moderating counterbalance to Islamic extremism. It is ready for a larger role in global affairs. It is a would-be peacemaker in the troubled Middle East. This is a trend that should be encouraged and supported with deft diplomacy by countries opposing the violent perversions of Islamic extremism.

The Case of Turkey

If Indonesia, population 202 million, is a successful example of a non-Arab land where Islam and democracy coexist, the next most striking example is Turkey, population 74 million. Like Indonesia, Turkey is Islamic, a democracy, but not an Arab country. Like Indonesia, it is a nation that could play a significant role in helping thwart Islamic extremism.

Turkey has long been seen as a land-bridge between East and West. For decades it has looked westward to Europe. In recent times, however, it has been refurbishing its ties with countries that border it, such as Iran, Iraq, and Syria. This includes plans to launch its own Arabic-language satellite TV station in an effort to connect with the Arab world.

In part this began as a reaction to the opposition of some European countries to Turkey's admission to the European Union. The opponents argued Turkey was not a European power.

In part it was because Turkey's new foreign minister, Ahmet Davutoglu, a former professor of international relations, believes in a policy of "zero problems with neighbors." As part of this philosophy, Turkey ended a 16-year freeze in relations with Armenia. Turkey has also granted more cultural and political rights to its 14-million-strong Kurdish minority in a bid to ease tensions not only with them but with Kurds in Iraq, Iran, and Syria.

Relations between Turkey and the United States dipped in 2003 when the Turkish parliament refused to permit transit of American troops through Turkey to open a second front in the war with Iraq. With the election of Obama to the American presidency, and his early visit to Turkey for a key outreach speech to the Muslim world, the relationship has regained warmth. President Obama termed Turkey a "critical" ally, declared that the United States was "not at war with Islam," and concluded his speech in parliament by kissing Turkish prime minister Recep Tayyip Erdogan on both cheeks.[8] President Obama's support for Turkey's bid for membership in the European Union also did not hurt.

Turkish officials were careful to explain that their renewed interest in the Muslim east did not mean a chill towards the West. But Israeli actions in Gaza drew an angry response from Turkey.

Eyebrows were raised in Washington over some unusually warm Turkish congratulations for Iranian president Mahmoud Ahmadinejad's questionable reelection, but other diplomats saw Turkey's pipeline to Iran useful for passing back-channel messages involved, for instance, with mediation of the Israeli-Palestinian conflict.

Indonesia and Turkey are powerful symbols for the Muslim world of the compatibility of democracy and Islam. They should be nurtured as important potential allies in the war of ideas with Islamic extremism.

For all its past anguish under Saddam Hussein, and the war thereafter, Iraq is limping towards democracy. With a free press, elections, and stabilization, in time, it too could become an example to the rest of the Arab world of concord between Islam and democracy. Over a longer and unpredictable time span even Pakistan, if it achieves stability, and although not an Arab country, could become another large country demonstrating concord between Islam and democracy. They are countries that could benefit from sophisticated U.S. public diplomacy.

PART
IV

What We Should Do

*"People who engage in terror do not want peace and
justice and people who want peace and justice
do not engage in terror."*

GEORGE P. SHULTZ

IN THE DECADE since USIA was dismantled, its remnants inserted into the Department of State, there have been more than 30 major reports and studies recommending solutions to what is widely recognized as a major failing in post–Cold War U.S. public diplomacy.

The Center for Strategic and International Studies, the Aspen Institute, the Heritage Foundation, the Council on Foreign Relations, the Public Diplomacy Council, the Rand Corporation, the Brookings Institution, and a string of other private and government-connected entities, have offered assessments of what should be done. Some have recommended major restructuring within the State Department. Some have recommended partnerships with private enterprise. Some have recommended most of the task being conducted by the private sector.

After the attacks on the United States of September 11, 2001, there was new urgency to the need for a robust campaign to communicate, particularly to the Muslim world, the truths about American principles, policies, and culture. The national commission appointed to make recommendations for enhancing national security to prevent future attacks declared: "Just as we did in the Cold War, we need to defend our ideals abroad vigorously. America does stand up for its values. The United States defended, and still defends, Muslims against tyrants and criminals in Somalia, Bosnia, Kosovo, Afghanistan, and Iraq. If the United States does not act aggressively to define itself in the Islamic world, the extremists will gladly do the job for us."

Lessons Learned

In 2005, former secretary of state George P. Shultz chaired a wide-ranging seminar in California bringing together a number of other former officials responsible for public diplomacy and experts on the Islamic world. The purpose was to examine lessons learned from the practice of public diplomacy—especially international broadcasting—in the Cold War and to suggest how the United States could "more effectively counter extremism, promote democracy, and improve understanding of itself in the Islamic world."

In setting the scene for discussion, Shultz cited polls cataloging anti-American sentiment in Muslim societies as suggesting the theme: "They hate us, what's wrong with us?" This, however, he said, should be reframed to: "They hate us, what's eating at their societies?"

The United States needs to persist, he said, "with the message that we stand for liberty and that we believe that liberty can flourish on Arab and Muslim soil. Our enemies (Iran, Syria, the rogues) need to be told this as often, and forcefully, as our friends in Egypt and Saudi Arabia. For decades we have accepted a terrible bargain with Arab and Muslim authoritarianism. On 9/11 we discovered that the bargain did not work. A public diplomacy worth the effort and the price tag must start from that recognition. . . . We have to state in unequivocal terms our belief in the necessity of modernity in Muslim lands."

The message from the seminar included several key points:

Lessons from the Cold War show that international broadcasting can have an important impact on today's problems.

Mainstream Muslims must take on the radicals. In the end, the Islamic community needs to engage in this battle. We need to encourage the effort. The mission is to "dry up the sea of support in which terrorists swim."

Monitor what people say and be ready to interact. The Middle East is the world center for conspiracy theories. A counter-conspiracy effort is needed, to be candid, open, and factually correct.

Place emphasis on the importance of work. Unemployment in some Muslim communities for men over 40 is more than 50 percent. Work connects people with reality.

Saudi Arabia, Egypt, and Iran need different messages. Each is different. (Saudi Arabia and Egypt have pro-American regimes with anti-American populations. In Iran the rulers are anti-American but the population is on the other side.)

Pay attention to women with content programming. In some countries they are kept out of everyday life, and have much time to watch TV at home where the morals police cannot get at them.

Put emphasis on basic education. Too much of what passes for education in Islamic lands is propaganda. Include special incentives to learn English.

Work with voices in the Arab world that carry encouraging and reasonable messages.

Our news content must be candid, tuned to local audiences, and remorselessly accurate. Credibility is the name of the game.

Lessons Not Learned

Sadly, there has been little evidence of the major reorganization and revitalization needed to mount a coherent and forceful public diplomacy campaign against the disinformation of Islamic extremism. In the face of this disarray, Al Qaeda and other terrorist groups have adopted increasingly sophisticated techniques in the media campaign which they recognize plays a key role in their violent campaign, against the United States and its allies.

In the presidential election campaign of 2008 there were hints that a new incumbent of the White House might move to reinvigorate public diplomacy. John McCain declared that if elected he would reinstate USIA as a separate and vigorous agency. While Barack Obama did not offer specifics, he said he would bolster the U.S. public diplomacy effort. But when the new administration took office, Secretary of State Hillary Clinton said she saw no need to reestablish USIA as a separate agency and would invigorate its mission from within the State Department.

President Obama's early speeches of outreach in Cairo and Ankara to the Muslim world were omens of a new approach. His message was sincere, his words eloquent, and his quotations from the Koran pertinent. He reached out beyond governments and political organizations to millions of ordinary Muslims.

The State Department amplified the message, translated into 14 languages on its website, posted on blogs, and sent by text message to mobile phones in more than 170 countries. The government's Middle East TV station, Alhurra, and the Voice of America radio network, gave the president's message major coverage.

But however much Arab listeners and viewers might have warmed to President Obama personally, this does not translate into more favorable views of the United States. After the president spoke, polls showed 82 percent of Palestinians still had an unfavorable view of the United States. Only 14 percent of Turks had a favorable view, and in Egypt only 27 percent of those polled had a favorable view of the United States.[1]

To be successful, public diplomacy cannot be a one-shot affair with a presidential speech. It demands a long-term strategy with follow-up, amplification, and explanation. Foreign audiences need interpretation of U.S. government policies and insight into the American way of life and love of freedom. In the heyday of USIA this would have been undertaken by skilled public affairs officers attached to American embassies around the world, usually versed in the languages and culture of their assigned countries and endowed with long-cultivated ties with local newspaper editors, TV directors, and other opinion-molders.

They were the eyes and ears of public diplomacy on the ground, listening to what was said about the United States and its policies, reporting this back to USIA headquarters in Washington, and recommending programs and visitations that would be effective for the regions in which they were based.

Today many of those positions are vacant, or being filled by junior officers. Language proficiency of officers in some Arab countries is either poor or nonexistent.

The officers no longer report to seasoned public diplomacy professionals in their own agency but to desk officers in the State Department. The undersecretary for public diplomacy in Washington does not handle budget or personnel decisions.

Many U.S. libraries and cultural centers which used to host large numbers of visitors in foreign cities have either been closed for security reasons or are now behind fortified defenses which discourage usage.

As various observers and entities have looked at the deficiencies of public diplomacy as practiced by the State Department, recommendations for improvement have been many. But none have been able to change a culture which in some cases does not understand the practice of public diplomacy and in some cases despises it as anathema to traditional diplomacy. Professional diplomats are groomed to deal with foreign governments or leaders, often in confidence, and holding their cards close to their chests. Practitioners of public diplomacy are trained to broadcast their messages far and wide, to mass audiences, or to thought-leaders able to influence mass audiences.

The integration of a culture of public diplomacy into the State Department has not been effective. A string of under-secretaries for public diplomacy, with little authority and slender resources, have been unable to make a difference.

There is no question that public diplomacy has in the past, and could again in the future, benefit from the wealth of ideas and resources from both major corporations and dedicated individuals. But to inspire various government agencies to cooperate in successful public diplomacy operations, and to articulate government policy successfully, a government agency must be the innovator and manager.

Thus the inevitable conclusion is that a renewed and vibrant U.S. public diplomacy effort requires a new and separate agency. It should replicate some of the best features and energy of the now-defunct USIA but embrace the new resources and skills for communicating with a world whose structure is changing politically and technologically. It should be staffed by men and women who have a passion for implementing the mission.

Critics may denounce the concept and cost of a new government agency. But the United States was able to spawn a new homeland security agency in time of need. A new public diplomacy agency has a role equally relevant to the long-term security of the United States. Dissuading a new generation of young men—and women—from lives of terrorism is so critical that even Secretary of Defense Robert Gates has pinpointed the huge discrepancy in funding between military operations and civilian public diplomacy, to the serious detriment of public diplomacy. For example, in Somalia the State Department's budget for public diplomacy is $30,000. The Pentagon's budget for the same purpose is $600,000.

Both Gates and Admiral Mike Mullen, chairman of the Joint Chiefs of Staff, have taken the rare step for military men of suggesting transfer of funds from the Defense Department to the State Department for public diplomacy. Unfortunately it is doubtful whether the State Department, after years of neglect and cutbacks, currently has the capacity and skills to effectively use such funds. The shortage of qualified and available foreign service officers has created a vacuum that is sometimes being filled with military personnel conducting development and public diplomacy tasks. By necessity, the Defense Department has stepped into public diplomacy areas the State Department has vacated. Congress has expressed concern about this rapid growth of the military's involvement in what was once the purview of the State Department. The House Appropriation Committee said many of the Pentagon's costlier programs appear as "alarmingly non-military propaganda, public relations, and behavioral modification messaging."[2]

Government departments rarely enthuse over the creation of new agencies likely to impinge on their own preserves, so the impetus for a new public diplomacy agency must come from Congress and the support of the presidency.

Republican senator Sam Brownback of Kansas introduced legislation that would have established a National Center for Strategic Communications, an agency very similar to the defunct USIA. "As America continues to fight the war on terrorism," said Brownback, "we cannot rely on military force alone to defeat the threat posed by Islamic extremism. While we spend a lot of time discussing tactics and troop deployments, we rarely analyze the broader ideological struggle."[3]

In addition to establishing a new public diplomacy agency, Brownback's plan would have abolished the lame undersecretary for public diplomacy position at the State Department, as well as the Broadcasting Board of Governors overseeing the Voice of America and other government radios. Their functions would be folded into the new National Center for Strategic Communications headed by a single director who would report directly to the president. This director would also preside over an interagency panel of all federal entities with missions involving strategic communications with foreign publics.

Though some of the Brownback proposals may be open to question, the senator made an essential point. To be effective, a strong public diplomacy operation requires a seat at the table with the president when foreign policy is being formulated. As Edward R. Murrow, USIA's first director, frequently opined, public diplomacy "must be in on the take-offs as well as the crash landings of foreign policy."

The Bush administration's decisions on torture, for instance, might have been modified if the president had heard an expert's well-sourced view on the likely torrent of negative reaction around the world. The president need not accept the advice from a director of public diplomacy, but the decision process would be helped by at least a discussion of the foreign opinion consequences of major foreign policy initiatives.

The proposed legislation from Senator Brownback was introduced in the waning days of the 110th Congress. The senator said he was waiting for a propitious time to reintroduce it.

There is a supportive lobby in Congress on the public diplomacy front. Republican senator Richard Lugar from Indiana, for example, says the United States is waging the battle of ideas with "one hand tied behind its back." He deplores the closing or drastic downsizing of "American Centers" throughout the world because of security concerns and budget constraints. He says the British and French attract throngs of students and young people, as the United States used to do, in major world cities with libraries, reading rooms, unfiltered internet access, film series, lectures, and language classes. Even Iran, said Lugar, has spread a network of 60 cultural centers in Asia, the Middle East, Africa, and Europe that offer Persian language courses and extensive library resources—and a platform for anti-American propaganda.

Saying it's "time for the U.S. to get back in the game of public diplomacy," Lugar called on the secretary of state to reestablish publicly accessible American Centers around the world, "maximizing their use."[4]

Senator Lugar was also the force behind such projects as the Science Envoy Program. Noting that the United States has produced more Nobel laureates in the sciences than any other country, he pushed legislation which authorizes the sending of prominent scientists to travel the world to engage their counterparts, deepening and developing partnerships in all areas of science and technology. The first three, chosen in 2009, were Dr. Bruce Alberts, chair of the Department of Biochemistry and Biophysics at the University of California, San Francisco; Algerian-born Dr. Elias Zerhouni, professor of Radiology and Biomedical Engineering at Johns Hopkins University; and Egyptian-born Dr. Ahmed Zewail, professor of Chemistry and Physics at the California Institute of Technology, Pasadena.

Agenda for Progress

Here is a program for a new and revitalized American public diplomacy effort—for a new agency dedicated to public diplomacy with a director of cabinet status.

1. Budget

Military spending dwarfs the current budget for public diplomacy. Congress should authorize a substantial increase for public diplomacy in all its forms. As an early advisory report declared: Needed is "an immediate end to the absurd and dangerous underfunding of public diplomacy in time of peril."

2. Journalists

Influential foreign journalists stationed in Washington should be cultivated for meaningful background briefings by senior government officials. Readers in Japan and India and Britain, for example, will place more reliance on interpretations of American foreign policy from their papers' and TV channels' own correspondents than from American news organizations.

Currently the State Department runs foreign press centers in Washington and New York. But they are more for facilitating run-of-the-mill foreign media needs and bringing in guest speakers. Reporters and columnists from the *New York Times* and the *Washington Post* and anchors from CNN are much more likely than the foreign press to gain exclusive access, tips, and on- or off-the-record sessions with top White House officials and cabinet ministers such as the secretary of state.

U.S. public diplomacy officials attached to U.S. embassies around the world cultivate and engage with newspaper editors and TV directors but reporters from those countries stationed in Washington or at the UN still have substantial credibility with their home offices in their interpretation of U.S. foreign policy.

Obviously, special Washington attention should be given to resident correspondents from Arab countries. Al Jazeera may not be the favorite network of any White House, but a savvy president or secretary of state engaging with its Washington bureau chief can successfully project his or her message on it instantly to millions of Muslim viewers.

3. Language

A crash program for training selected public diplomacy officers in Arabic and other high-priority languages should be launched. Financial and other incentives should be offered for service in Arab, or particularly dangerous, countries.

4. Exchanges

Three years after creating the USIA, President Eisenhower launched the People-to-People program within the agency, declaring: "I have long believed, as have many before me, that peaceful relations between nations requires understanding and mutual respect between individuals.

"Over the years, people-to-people exchanges have proved one of the most successful aspects of public diplomacy. Even during the Cold War, the United States and the Soviet Union exchanged 50,000 citizens over 30 years." A House foreign affairs committee found that "contact with America and Americans reduces anti-Americanism. Visitors, particularly students, have more positive views about America than non visitors by 10 percentage points."

Today 45 percent of the world's population is under 25. Reaching that student-age bracket with positive contacts with Americans is a particular objective of both the U.S. government and various private-sector institutions. Others brought to America under the exchange programs include veteran judges and journalists and artists and politicians and people from various professions.

Government funding for exchanges totaled $635 million in 2010, up from $538 million the previous year. That covers a range of exchange programs, from the Fulbright program to the International Visitor Program, with guests from countries as diverse as Ireland and Tibet. If there were one way to improve the programs, it would be to expand them. Thomas Pickering, a hard-headed former ambassador to a number of countries, testified before a congressional committee that the international exchange programs should be doubled.

Some years ago, the newspaper I was editing participated in a program to bring about a dozen editors a year from various countries to America to sharpen their professional skills and expose them to the American way of life. Initially, the program focused on editors from Eastern Europe and Russia who had been brought up under Communism but expanded to include editors from Africa and Asia. Each editor spent a month at an American newspaper, and a week in Washington and a week in New York. We took an editor a year from such countries as Serbia, Kosovo, former Soviet Georgia, and the Sudan. They spent a month in our newsroom following a program of their choice and special interests. But when the days were done we did not ship them off to the isolation of hotel rooms but to the homes of our staffers who had volunteered to house them. Thus, they went with their host families to supermarkets, boy scout meetings, town-government meetings, and high school football games; they rode horses and watched American TV. For our staff it was a huge educational experience about the countries from which our guests came. For the visitors, it was an eye-opening view of the United States. We engaged in long discussions with our guests, sometimes into the wee hours. Discussion was often robust about U.S. foreign policies. While some left unconvinced about the wisdom of those policies, without exception they took away a positive view of America and Americans. For years afterwards they would keep in touch, e-mailing us about problems in journalism, or with their governments, but also communicating about births and marriages and other family events.

If there were one thing that would have improved the program, it would have been to host, say, a hundred visiting editors a year instead of twelve.

It is difficult to underestimate the value of university student exchanges. The number of international students at colleges and universities in the United States reached an all-time high of more than 670,000 in 2009. About 98,000 of them were from China. Meanwhile President Obama has committed to raise the number of American students studying in China from 20,000 to 100,000 over four years.

Clearly, people-to-people exchanges are a winning program. They should be expanded. Private organizations engaged in them should be praised and supported.

5. Culture

Diplomacy, as former secretary of state George P. Shultz suggests, can be likened to gardening—"You get the weeds out when they are small. You also build confidence and understanding. Then, when a crisis arises, you have a solid basis from which to work."[5]

Thus the role of cultural diplomacy. The Advisory Committee on Cultural Diplomacy to the State Department asserts, is to plant seeds: "ideas and ideals; aesthetic strategies and devices; philosophical and political arguments; spiritual perceptions; ways of looking at the world—which may flourish in foreign soils. Cultural diplomacy reveals the soul of a nation." American art, dance, film, music, and literature continue to inspire people the world over despite political differences. Cultural diplomacy, the advisory committee suggests, "demonstrates our values, and combats the popular notion that Americans are shallow, violent, and godless."[6]

The State Department's unit for promoting cultural diplomacy relies on some 1,500 private sector organizations, academic institutions, and nongovernmental organizations (NGOs) to manage the majority of its programs sending artists and musicians, dancers and filmmakers, abroad. But government resources, both money and personnel, for cultural diplomacy are insufficient. With vacancies in the ranks of public diplomacy officials posted to embassies around the world, many cultural diplomacy officers have been transferred to noncultural slots and the bureaucratic administrative tasks that regular public diplomacy officers would carry out. The committee cites the opinion of a senior Egyptian government official: "We've had a cultural agreement with the United States since 1962. Why not implement it? We want people to know about real Americans. You have the right to be different, and I have the right to be different. Let your people know that Egyptians are not just fanatics—Islam is one religion, but there are many ways of applying it. I won't let what happened in Abu Ghraib change my feelings for the American people. My idea of America is the Statue of Liberty opening her arms, not turning away. Americans should build bridges. . . . They need to open up again. Don't go into a shell."[7]

Culture can go where politics might not. A symphony orchestra is welcomed in North Korea where a Congressional delegation might not be.

A new public diplomacy agency should encourage more Arab and Muslim artists, performers, and writers to be invited to the United States, and more of their American counterparts to be encouraged to visit the Islamic world.

6. Religion

Americans are a religious people.

Muslims are a religious people.

105

But in the past there has been some reticence on the part of the U.S. government about injecting religious faith too prominently into its public diplomacy programs.

This should not be. Much of the confrontation between Islam and the West is directly attributable to religion. To advance religious freedom in the world, the U.S. Congress in 1998 enacted the International Religious Freedom Act requiring an ambassador-at-large for international religious freedom and creating an Office of International Religious Freedom in the State Department.

The United States does not have a national religion. One of the plaints of some Muslims is that Americans do not listen enough to the audiences with which they seek engagement. That necessarily requires at least a modest understanding of Islam. Muslims should understand that that necessarily involves examination of the interpretations of the Koran used to inspire Islamic extremism and violence. This is an area in which moderate Muslim communities in the United States could communicate constructively to non-Muslims.

Americans, meanwhile, should understand that discussions about their own faiths with Muslims are reasonable, but sensitive. Some Arab lands take an uncompromising position against conversion of Muslims to other, and particularly Christian, faiths.

However there is no reason why U.S. public diplomacy should not have a deft role in the same kind of international interfaith conferences arranged by moderate Islamic countries such as Indonesia and even Saudi Arabia.

Nongovernmental organizations such as the Washington-based International Center for Religion and Diplomacy, have had some quiet but successful faith-based reconciliation negotiations in such tough countries as the Sudan, Afghanistan, Pakistan, and even Iran. Freedom of religion is one of the basic freedoms that Americans cherish for themselves. We should not be bashful about supporting it for others.

7. Sports

If American music can go where politics cannot, so can sports. The National Basketball Association (NBA) continues its pioneer efforts to export the game of basketball worldwide. As part of its "Basketball Without Borders" program, it hosts clinics and development camps and arranges games in countries such as China. It also recruits star players like Yao Ming, the Chinese center, from their own countries to play for U.S. teams. More than 80 international players began the 2009 season on NBA rosters.

In a remarkable breakthrough, the NBA in 2009 invited the Iranian national basketball team to play in Utah and Texas. When the team played in Salt Lake City, where there is a sizeable group of Iranian expatriates, Iranian and American flags fluttered throughout the stadium as followers cheered on both American and Iranian players.

Time reported that 56 American softball players traveled to Cuba in late 2009 for a series of goodwill games that "probably did more for America's public image than any single political effort over the past 50 years."

In Nicaragua, where political relations with the United States have frayed ever since former revolutionary Daniel Ortega came back to power in 2007, U.S. ambassador Robert Callahan discovered he could do some of his best work wearing a baseball mitt. "I think the State Department is coming to realize, belatedly, that baseball can be a very effective tool in public diplomacy," he told *Time*.

Where sport can play a role in breaking down political barriers, it should be encouraged.

8. Women

As intellectuals and reformers from Morocco to Iraq debate the changes that must come to their world, particularly significant is the discourse about the role of women in Islamic societies. It is significant because the emergence of women from the subordinate role to which many of them have been relegated in Islamic countries would speed the economic and political progress of these lands. A UN report prepared by Arab scholars found that stunting the education and advancement of women is a major hindrance to development. One in every two Arab women can neither read nor write. As the report concluded: "Society as a whole suffers when half of its productive potential is stifled."[8]

There are some pitfalls to be negotiated as public diplomacy addresses the audience of Arab women. While many want to achieve a stronger role in their societies, their strategy may be contained within the Islamic theology of *sharia,* the body of Islamic law developed over the years by religious scholars to provide moral guidance to Muslims.

Isobel Coleman, an expert on women in Islam, says that *sharia* is open to a range of understanding and that "progressive Muslims are seeking to interpret its rules to accommodate a modern role for women." In many Islamic countries, says Coleman, reformers have abandoned futile attempts to replace *sharia* with secular law. They are trying to promote women's rights within an Islamic framework, which "seems more likely to succeed, since it fights theology with theology, a natural strategy in countries with conservative populations and where religious authority is hard to challenge."[9]

This involves sensitivity but should not dull U.S. public diplomacy advocating the evolution of Muslim women in education, business, and politics.

Free agents like Greg Mortenson, author of *Three Cups of Tea,* have proved that where there is security there is a hunger for education among women. The American mountaineer turned school-builder has built 80 schools in Afghanistan, many of them focusing on the education of girls. More important than troop levels or war budgets, he says, is winning trust at the local levels through relationships evolving slowly, literally over cups of tea.

9. Broadcasting

In the history of U.S. government public diplomacy, international broadcasting has played a critical and illustrious role.

When I was a foreign correspondent in Africa and Asia, the most valued part of my kit after my portable typewriter was a shortwave radio. It was my link to the outside world in the remotest parts of those continents. Across the static over thousands of miles, I would tune in each night (when reception was best) to the Voice of America. It gave me a reliable account of what was happening in America and elsewhere in the world.

Years later, when I served as director of VOA in the Reagan administration, my respect for VOA was heightened by personal contact with the talented journalists, foreign service officers, and expatriates from various lands who so professionally gathered the news and broadcast it around the world in a multitude of tongues.

Radio Liberty and Radio Free Europe broadcast to the Soviet Union and its captive satellite countries, respectively, with news withheld from them of what was going on in their own lands.

There is no question that these radios gave heart to citizens behind the Iron Curtain and played an important role in their ultimate march to freedom.

VOA was loosely controlled under the mantle of USIA, but after the demise of USIA in 1999, the radios came under the authority of a new entity, the Broadcasting Board of Governors (BBG), which provided oversight of all the government's nonmilitary international broadcasting. In addition to VOA, Radio Free Europe, and Radio Liberty, this now includes Radio and TV Marti (to Cuba), Radio Free Asia, Alhurra TV and Radio Sawa (to Arab countries), and Radio Farda (to Iran).

The idea was that the BBG would provide a firewall between the radios and other government public diplomacy units, guaranteeing the journalistic independence, and thus credibility, of the radios.

It has not proved a happy chapter in the story of U.S. international broadcasting. Although designed to be politically impartial, evenly divided between Republicans and Democrats, the BBG underwent a period of blatantly political influence.

Instead of providing oversight, it intruded into management of individual radio services, determining services what languages should be retained or dropped. It canceled broadcasts in languages the professional broadcasters considered essential, withholding funding from some and adding it to others not favored by the professionals. It canceled VOA's Arab-language service on the grounds that Alhurra TV and Radio Sawa were adequate broadcasters to the Arab world. It canceled VOA's Russian-language service twelve days before Russia invaded Georgia. Eventually membership of the eight-person board dwindled to the point where a quorum, and thus its utility, was problematical.

Many of the broadcasters hoped that with the advent of the Obama administration, there might be a housecleaning, even the abolition of the board, replacing it with a single director of broadcasting. After a year's delay, the administration replaced the old board, nominating eight new members, four Republicans and four Democrats, to undergo confirmation by the U.S. Senate in 2010, the chair being Walter Isaacson, a respected former CEO of CNN and editor of *Time*.

The U.S. Senate approved a budget of $746 million for all broadcasting in the board's coming year, $204 million of that for the flagship VOA. But the Senate and House report accompanying budget approval warned sharply of the need to maintain services in key languages, especially VOA English and services in various other languages which the old board had wanted to cut. It thus appeared that VOA would retain English frequencies it might otherwise have lost. VOA broadcasters had argued that English remains a critical language for reaching leaders of countries where English is not the universal language.

The new board faces an unenviable list of challenges.

It must determine whether there is technical overlapping between some services and whether shared transmitter costs, for example, could cut costs.

It must determine whether, with the rapid growth of private Arab TV networks such as Al Jazeera and Al Aribya, the U.S. government's Alhurra is an effective competitor.

It must decide whether, in light of small listening and viewing audiences in Cuba, Radio Marti and TV Marti should continue to exist in their present form.

It must tackle the problem of overlapping broadcasting with other government entities.

The State Department is pursuing its own radio programming to Afghanistan. The Defense Department has made public diplomacy and broadcasting a major ethos of military operations.

The new BBG members must help reconcile VOA's charter obligation to broadcast accurate, objective, and balanced news about America and the world, while often pressured by congressional critics to give more weight to its other requirement of explaining U.S. policies.

The BBG must also determine the U.S. government's balance between radio broadcasting, which is still the informational lifeline for millions around the world, with television, which has become the news provider for many in the Arab world. There is also the power of the internet's social media to engage in a dialogue with a vast audience of friends and foes around the globe. Each medium now plays an important role in the practice of public diplomacy,

With new minds and voices on the BBG, it should be given a chance to rectify the mistakes and confusion of the recent past. The broadcasters deserve better. If this proves not to be the case, Congress should consider a new formula for direction and oversight.

10. Listening

While the radios do some polling to find out how many people in various countries are listening to, or looking at, their radio and TV programming, this research may be helpful to the broadcasters but does not go into any particular depth about what people are thinking.

When USIA was an agency determining its own destiny, it polled extensively in order to plumb foreign opinion about the United States and U.S. policies. Research from this and other sources helped tailor public diplomacy programs to specifically targeted populations in particular countries and regions.

Several factors have combined to produce far less of such information. Budget cuts are one such factor. Another is the thinner line of experienced public affairs officers abroad who took their own soundings, mingled with thought-leaders and opposition politicians as well government figures, and sent back to Washington sophisticated analyses of the public mood in their assigned countries. A third factor is the sharp decline of foreign reporting by the American media, which used to provide an additional viewpoint of public and governmental opinion in the nations they were covering. In hard economic times, foreign news bureaus are the first expense news organizations cut.

Thus, a plaint from some foreigners today is that America does too little listening and too much lecturing. If Congress decides to seriously tackle the disarray of current U.S. public diplomacy, a priority program should be for polling, and supplementary collection by public affairs officers, of foreign opinion helpful in countering misinformation and deliberate misrepresentation.

Conclusions

The war the United States is fighting against Islamic extremism necessarily requires both military force and "soft power," the phrase that has come to mean a nonmilitary mix of economic development, humanitarian effort, and public diplomacy.

Military force achieves its goal by coercion. Soft power achieves its goal by persuasion.

This book has concerned itself mainly with the public diplomacy dimension of soft power, which the author considers to be critical in the campaign under way. I am not alone. From Secretary of Defense Robert Gates down through an array of his commanders we have heard pleas for vigorous public diplomacy in support of military victory. As General Stanley McChrystal, the U.S. commander in Afghanistan, tersely put it: "The information domain is a battlespace." The U.S. and its allies must "take aggressive actions to win the important battle of perception."[10]

The problem is this: the U.S. military is arguably the most powerful and effective in the world. By contrast, the U.S. public diplomacy machine is in disarray. Unwisely dismantled after the Cold War in which it had played a significant role, its remnants have been starved of resources and manpower. Its annual budget has hovered somewhere less than 1 percent of the military's.

The enemy the U.S. military faces today is not the set-piece divisions of Germany in World War II or the Soviet Union's armada of nuclear weapons in the Cold War. It is a shadowy band of un-uniformed zealots with deadly intent who have managed to disperse their operations to franchises in Somalia and Yemen and Mali and Nigeria and even Europe and America. The military targets these die-hard terrorists. Public diplomacy seeks to engage moderate Muslims and persuade them that there is a better, nonviolent way to end the poverty and tribulation upon which terrorism so often breeds.

During the U.S. presidential campaign of 2008, John McCain charged that the abolition of USIA by the Clinton presidency and Congress "amounted to unilateral disarmament in the war of ideas." He said if elected he would work with Congress to create a new independent agency as a "critical element in combating Islamic extremism."

As president, Obama elected not to go down that route but instead embark on a personal odyssey of public diplomacy. He delivered conciliatory words to the Muslim lands of the Middle East which were, for the most part, initially well received. But public diplomacy requires consistency and long-term follow-up by its on-the-ground practitioners, offering specific programs of engagement, and cultural exchanges, and demonstrations of goodwill. It needs an infrastructure with funding and personnel skilled at deflecting myths about America and establishing trust and long-lasting friendships.

The role of the Department of State is to manage the foreign policy of the United States, as defined by the president and debated with Congress. The officers who arrive in the department's topmost ranks are smart, impressive, and tough when needs be. Their clientele is foreign diplomats and government leaders, both friends and foes. Public diplomacy is not their primary interest or training. Nor has the introverted State Department, since acquiring the remnants of USIA, proved spectacular at running an inherently extroverted public diplomacy operation.

History argues for a new and independent agency committed, with singular focus, to public diplomacy and headed by a director of cabinet rank who has the ear of the president on issues of foreign policy.

Good though the old USIA was at its zenith, the new agency should not be a carbon copy of the old.

As an American government agency, its watchword should be "leverage." It should encourage others to magnify and multiply its own efforts. It should be the catalyst, motivating other agencies, entities, foundations, nations, and the American people, to take constructive measures alone, or in partnerships, for worthy American goals.

On the home front, government departments ranging from those involved in trade and commerce and economic and humanitarian aid, to the Peace Corps, the Department of Defense, with its enormous capability for postaction construction, and the State Department, with its handling of visas for foreign students and performing artists, should have their international programs coordinated under the mantle of public diplomacy.

Involvement of a myriad of NGOs and foundations and many others already active in international training and exchange programs could be enhanced and expanded. Major corporations with global interests might share some of their resources, their marketing expertise, and research of foreign cultures.

Many individual Americans are already generous in hosting foreign visitors. Others, if made aware of the need, could become an army of volunteers. The Smith-Mundt Act, which precludes U.S. government public diplomacy departments from projecting internally what they project abroad, should be revisited. Private citizens made more aware of their country's public diplomacy efforts and needs might volunteer to help. They might become private ambassadors of public diplomacy when they travel abroad on business or pleasure.

The sizable Muslim communities in the United States should similarly be encouraged to play more active roles in constructive dialogue with Muslim countries abroad.

Internationally, moderate Muslim, but non-Arab, nations such as Indonesia and Turkey could in time become influential interlocutors in Middle Eastern disputes. Indonesia has indicated interest in a larger international role. Turkey is widening its contacts with neighboring Arab lands. U.S. public diplomacy should be as active as possible in such countries in explaining American policies, culture, and life.

Though much of U.S. public diplomacy is currently targeted at the Arab world, old friends such as Britain and France and other European nations should be nurtured. There are many cultural and emotional ties that bind with the United States and should be tended. Such countries could be more helpful in multilateral groupings or even as individual nations, for example, promoting democracy in lands where similar moves by the United States might be less welcome. The European Union appears to be gaining in stature and could be similarly helpful.

A new U.S. public diplomacy agency should retain its basic programs that have proved so successful. These include exchanges, particularly scholastic, scientific, cultural, and sport exchanges.

Skilled public diplomacy officers stationed abroad, versed in the culture and proficient in the languages of the countries they are assigned to, are the shock troops of the agency. They are first to detect trends, or negative developments, the eyes and ears of Washington, and innovative in suggesting programs most successful for their particular geographic area. Such a resource is critical.

The Voice of America is a brand of enormous value. It should remain the cornerstone of U.S. government international broadcasting, by both radio and TV. There could be some rearrangement from time to time of the other government broadcasting services as changing circumstances require. Clear messaging around the globe—a respected and independent news service, with intelligent discussion of U.S. foreign policy—balanced between radio, TV, and internet platforms, depending on the audiences targeted, is a continuing essential.

But embrace of "social media" and other developing communications techniques must be used to reach young audiences who acquire information 24/7 on small, metallic handheld devices.

What is the underlying theme for the message that America must project to the rest of the world? It is that its own rich heritage of freedom is something to which all humankind is entitled. This was the message of John F. Kennedy as he proclaimed unity with Berliners, of Ronald Reagan as he demanded that the Berlin wall be torn down.

As a foreign correspondent, I spent a good deal of time in Indonesia, witnessing its progression to democracy after years of autocratic rule under Sukarno. The students who spearheaded the campaign had never lived in a democratic state, but like people everywhere they knew instinctively that freedom was something to be grasped and nurtured.

Early in his presidency, President George W. Bush demonstrated that furthering liberty around the world was central to his foreign policy. For his second inaugural address he told his speechwriter that he wanted a "freedom" speech. The address contained 49 references to "freedom," "free," or "liberty." He addressed the choice between "oppression which is always wrong, and freedom which is eternally right." He declared: "Eventually, the call of freedom comes to every mind and soul. We do not accept the possibility of permanent slavery. Liberty will come to those who love it."[11]

Why then did a Bush administration initiative that promoted such goals for the Arab world get shot down barely after takeoff by governing regimes of countries whose citizens might most have benefited from it? The "Greater Middle East Initiative," as it was called, sought to have other industrialized nations join the United States in promoting economic development, political freedom, equality for women, and other democratic institutions in the Middle East. Criticism of the Bush plan came swiftly from influential Arab leaders who claimed it was being imposed on them heavy-handedly. Egypt's President Hosni Mubarak, whose own regime would have been obliged to make major concessions to democracy, charged the Bush administration as behaving "as if the region and its states do not exist, as if they have no sovereignty over their land, no ownership."

It is naïve to suggest that Arabs are a branch of humankind untouched by the desire for freedom. As non-Arab countries such as Indonesia have proved, and Arab countries such as Iraq may demonstrate in time, Islam and democracy are not incompatible. In various Arab lands, intellectuals and brave reformers are watching, waiting, and working for the constructive changes of which they dream.

A good Muslim friend of mine, a former cabinet-level official from the Sudan, now a professor in the United States, argues that reform must be his own Arab people's initiative and cannot be imposed on them. He recommends roundtable talks with religious and political leaders in the region seeking response and dialogue. The Islamic concepts of consultation (*shura*), consensus (*ijima*), and independent interpretive judgement (*ijitihad*) are totally compatible, he says, with democracy. Nor, I remind him, are they totally alien to practitioners of public diplomacy.

However democracy advances in the Arab world, and however its ultimate character differs from Jeffersonian democracy as Americans know it, the quest for freedom is noble and should remain the underlying premise of U.S. public diplomacy.

From President Bush's inaugural address a final line: "The only force powerful enough to stop the rise of tyranny and terror, and replace hatred with hope, is the force of human freedom."

NOTES

PART I: The Rise and Fall of USIA

1. The letter was obtained by coalition forces in Iraq and made public by the office of the U.S. director of national intelligence, which said the U.S. government had the "highest confidence" in its authenticity.

2. Department of State, "Report of the President's Task Force on U.S. Government International Broadcasting," December, 1991.

3. Ibid.

4. Ibid.

5. Ibid.

6. Ibid.

7. Ibid.

8. Ibid.

9. Ibid.

10. Department of State, "Commission on Broadcasting to the People's Republic of China," September, 1992.

11. Ibid.

12. Ibid.

13. Nicholas J. Cull, *The Cold War and the USIA*, New York: Cambridge University Press, 2008, p. 431.

14. *9/11 Commission Report*, New York: Barnes and Noble, 2004, Ch. 12.

15. Council on Foreign Relations, "Independent Task Force Report on Terrorism," New York, 2001.

16. Council on Foreign Relations, "Report on Finding America's Voice," New York, 2003.

17. Department of State, "Djerjian Advisory Group Report on Public Diplomacy for the Arab and Muslim World," 2003.

18. U.S. Government Accountability Office, "U.S. Public Diplomacy," 2005.

19. U.S. Government Accountability Office, "U.S. Public Diplomacy," 2006.

20. U.S. Government Accountability Office, "U.S. Public Diplomacy," 2007.

21. U.S. Government Accountability Office, "U.S. Public Diplomacy," 2009.

22. John McCain, "An Enduring Peace Built on Freedom," *Foreign Affairs*, November–December, 2007, 19–34.

23. Quoted in Walter Pincus, *Washington Post*, January 19, 2009.

24. Talk Radio News Service release, October 15, 2009.

25. Voice of America Charter.

26. U.S. Government Accountability Office, "Broadcasting to Cuba," 2009.

27. Center on Public Diplomacy, "An Evaluation of Alhurra Television Programming," University of Southern California, 2008.

28. Broadcasting Board of Governors, press release on Alhurra, December 11, 2008.

PART II: Indonesia:
Where Democracy and Islam Coexist

Much of the material in this segment is from on-scene reportage in Indonesia by John Hughes while a correspondent for the *Christian Science Monitor*. His dispatches, supplemented by additional research and interviews over time, were also the basis of a book, *Indonesian Upheaval*, published by the David McKay Company, New York, in 1967. The book was published in Britain and Australia by Angus and Robertson, London, in 1968 under the title *The End of Sukarno*. The book was republished with a new preface under the same title in 2002 by Archipelago Press/Editions, Didier Millet, of Singapore.

PART III: Indonesia: An Example for Islam?

1. Joshua Kurlantzick, *Boston Globe*, September 10, 2009.
2. Sidney Jones, Reuters, January 14, 2010.
3. Leekuan Yew, "The US, Iraq, and the War on Terror." *Foreign Affairs*, January–February, 2007, pp. 2–7.
4. Hassan Wirajuda, *New York Times*, June 8, 2007.
5. Susilo Bambang Yudhoyono, *Economist World Survey*, 2010.
6. Robert D. Kaplan, *Atlantic On-line*, February 13, 2009.
7. Quoted in John Hughes, *Christian Science Monitor*, November 15, 2009.
8. John Hughes, *Christian Science Monitor*, May 10, 2009.

PART IV: What We Should Do

1. Fouad Ajami, *Wall Street Journal*, November 30, 2009.
2. Quoted in Walter Pincus, *Washington Post*, July 28, 2009.
3. Sam Brownback, press release, September 23, 2008.
4. Richard Lugar, *Foreign Policy*, February 26, 2009.
5. Department of State, "Report of Advisory Committee on Cultural Diplomacy," September, 2005.
6. Ibid.
7. Ibid.
8. UN Development Program. "Arab Human Development Report," New York, 2004.
9. Isobel Coleman, "Women, Islam, and the New Grace." *Foreign Affairs*, January–February, 2006, pp. 24–38.
10. Quoted in Walter Pincus, *Washington Post*, September 27, 2009.
11. Quoted in John Hughes, *Christian Science Monitor*, September 6, 2006.

ABOUT THE AUTHOR

John Hughes is a Pulitzer-prize–winning journalist and former editor of the *Christian Science Monitor*.

He is currently a professor of international communications at Brigham Young University. He writes a nationally syndicated column for the *Christian Science Monitor*.

Born in Wales, educated in England, Hughes served for six years as the *Christian Science Monitor*'s Africa correspondent and six years as Far East correspondent, before becoming editor for nine years.

He was a Nieman Fellow at Harvard and won the Pulitzer prize for his coverage of Indonesia. He is a former president of the American Society of Newspaper Editors.

During the Reagan administration he served successively as associate director of USIA; director of the Voice of America; and assistant secretary of state for public affairs and State Department spokesman. In 1995 he served a one-year term at the UN as assistant secretary general and director of communications.

During the George H. W. Bush administration he chaired the President's Bipartisan Task Force on the Future of Government International Broadcasting and subsequently the Joint Presidential/Congressional Commission on Broadcasting to the People's Republic of China.

OTHER BOOKS BY JOHN HUGHES

THE NEW FACE OF AFRICA

INDONESIAN UPHEAVAL

AMERICA'S DIALOGUE WITH THE WORLD (contributor)

Herbert and Jane Dwight
Working Group on
Islamism and the
International Order

The Herbert and Jane Dwight Working Group on Islamism and the International Order seeks to engage in the task of reversing Islamic radicalism through reforming and strengthening the legitimate role of the state across the entire Muslim world. Efforts will draw on the intellectual resources of an array of scholars and practitioners from within the United States and abroad, to foster the pursuit of modernity, human flourishing, and the rule of law and reason in Islamic lands—developments that are critical to the very order of the international system.

The Working Group is chaired by Hoover fellows Fouad Ajami and Charles Hill with an active participation of Director John Raisian. Current core membership includes Russell A. Berman, Abbas Milani, and Shelby Steele, with contributions from Zeyno Baran, Reuel Marc Gerecht, Ziad Haider, John Hughes, Nibras Kazimi, Habib Malik, and Joshua Teitelbaum.

INDEX